Celebrity Chefs Across America

The Ingredients for Managing Diabetes

Written by Anthony Dias Blue
of *Bon Appétit* Magazine

Anthony Dias Blue is one of the most widely read and listened to food and wine personalities in the United States. His work reaches more than fifty million consumers each month. He can be found in print, radio, bookstores and in cyberspace. Among his many books are the popular cookbooks America's Kitchen *and* Thanksgiving Dinner. *Since January 1981, Anthony has been Wine & Spirits Editor of* Bon Appétit, *the largest circulation food publication in the United States.*

BROUGHT TO YOU BY SMITHKLINE BEECHAM PHARMACEUTICALS, MAKERS OF
Avandia®
rosiglitazone maleate

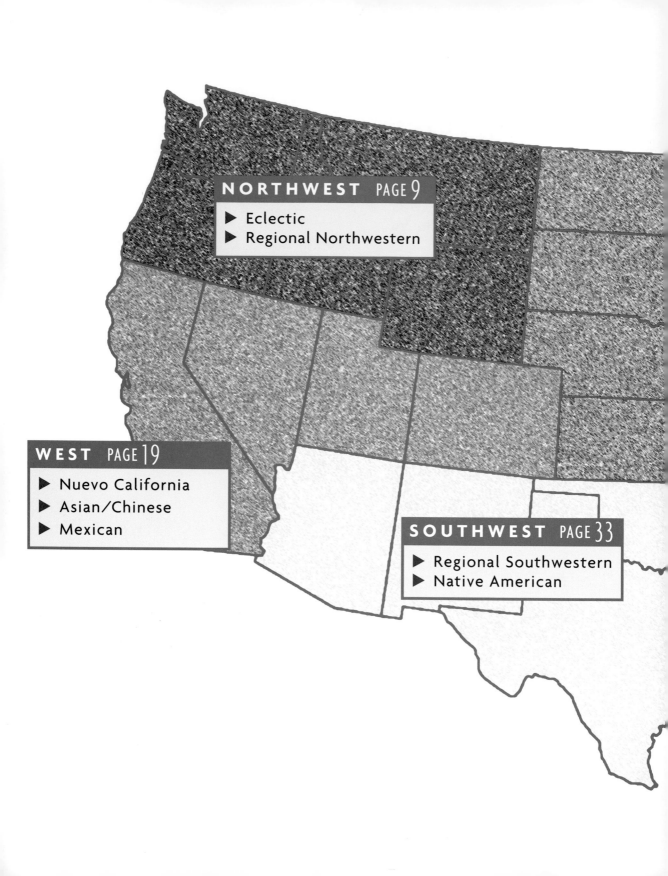

NORTHWEST PAGE 9
- ▶ Eclectic
- ▶ Regional Northwestern

WEST PAGE 19
- ▶ Nuevo California
- ▶ Asian/Chinese
- ▶ Mexican

SOUTHWEST PAGE 33
- ▶ Regional Southwestern
- ▶ Native American

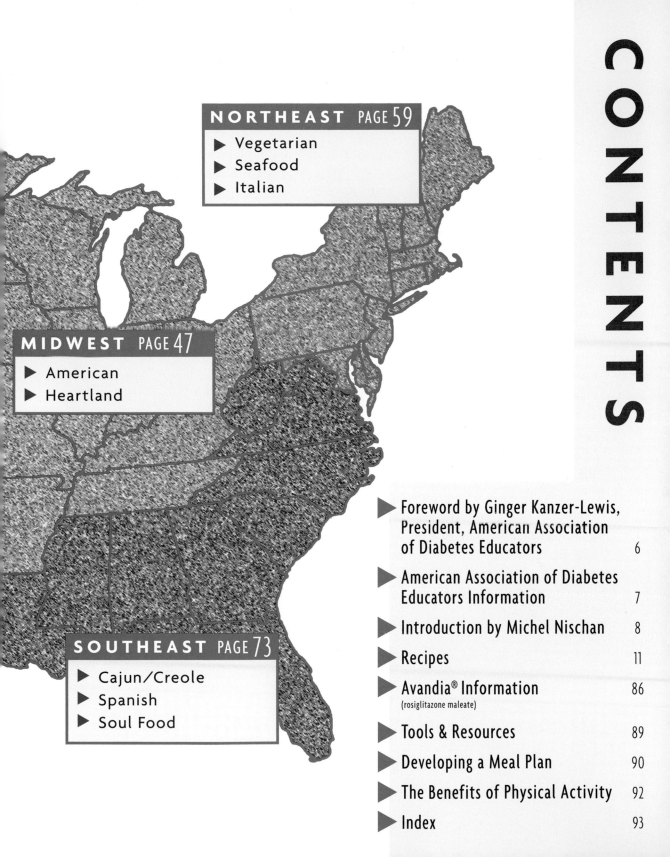

CONTENTS

▶FOREWORD
BY GINGER KANZER-LEWIS, AADE

As a diabetes educator and now President of the American Association of Diabetes Educators (AADE), I am all too familiar with the challenges diabetes can pose to people with diabetes and their families. The development of a proper diabetes management plan can pave the way for better overall health and independence in lifestyle choices. The AADE is an organization of healthcare professionals who are dedicated to improving the quality of diabetes education and care. Our commitment is to help people with diabetes, through education and care, live full and productive lives. I like to say that we are the people who take care of the people with diabetes.

Diabetes self-management means taking charge of diabetes with proper nutrition, exercise, good blood sugar control, treating insulin resistance and talking to your healthcare team. The AADE recognizes education as the heart of good diabetes self-management. Individuals, as well as their families and friends, should work with diabetes educators, and their healthcare team, to develop individualized meal plans and exercise routines, learn about proper medications and receive counseling for the challenges of a diabetes lifestyle. Please remember that in diabetes, self-management really matters!

Celebrity chefs from across the U.S. have joined forces to develop this unique cookbook that provides healthy recipes that fit into any diabetes self-management plan without compromising taste or heritage. As you will see, these diabetes-friendly recipes truly capture the flavors and flare of America, while maintaining an appropriate nutritional balance. We hope you will use this cookbook as a tool in the overall management of your diabetes.

Bon Appétit!

Ginger Kanzer-Lewis RNC, EdM, CDE
President
American Association of Diabetes Educators

The American Association of Diabetes Educators (AADE) is a multidisciplinary organization representing over 11,000 healthcare professionals who provide diabetes education and care. Members of the AADE are dedicated to improving the quality of diabetes education and care.

▶ AMERICAN ASSOCIATION OF DIABETES EDUCATORS INFORMATION

MISSION

The American Association of Diabetes Educators (AADE) is dedicated to promoting the role of the diabetes educator and to improving the quality of diabetes education and care.

MEMBERSHIP

The AADE is a multidisciplinary organization representing over 11,000 healthcare professionals who provide diabetes education and care. Members include nurses, dietitians, pharmacists, physicians, podiatrists, exercise physiologists, mental health professionals and social workers.

KEY GOALS

The AADE strives to advance the recognition of diabetes education as central to diabetes care. It is actively involved in support of funding for health initiatives promoting access to healthcare, creating quality standards for the performance and measurement of diabetes self-management education and expansion of Medicare benefits for beneficiaries of diabetes.

NATIONAL CAMPAIGN

Through its "Self-Management Matters" nationwide visibility campaign, the AADE works to promote the role of education and self-management. To date, tens of thousands of people with diabetes have been put in touch with diabetes educators in their area through the AADE awareness line — 800-TEAMUP4.

EDUCATION AND RESEARCH FOUNDATION

The AADE Education and Research Foundation is dedicated to improving the quality of life of all persons with diabetes by providing funds for research and program development in diabetes education. Through partnerships and memorial gift programs, the Foundation is able to provide funding for research in the field of diabetes education.

PUBLIC AWARENESS

Through research partnerships with healthcare industry firms, public awareness of essential industry and product information is passed along to patients for better understanding of the resources that are available.

▶ INTRODUCTION

ONE OF THE MAJOR CHALLENGES of living with diabetes is finding healthy foods that are flavorful. The good news is that healthy foods <u>can</u> taste good — it's all in the preparation.

When I was asked to rally top chefs from coast to coast for this cookbook, *Celebrity Chefs Across America — The Ingredients for Managing Diabetes*, I thought it would be a great opportunity to provide people with diabetes and their families with a resource for preparing delicious, healthy meals.

My passion for healthy cooking began with the devastating news that my five year-old son Chris had type 1 diabetes. I learned that millions of adults also suffer with type 2 diabetes and that, like Chris, the foods they eat have everything to do with their quality of life. I felt compelled to respond to the needs of other families living with diabetes and my cooking-style today revolves around creating dishes that help people with treatable illnesses thrive.

As Executive Chef of New York's *Heartbeat*, I am dedicated to creating a healthy, unique cuisine for my customers. Customers are grateful to have a menu filled with healthy foods and exciting flavors.

Celebrity Chefs Across America celebrates our nation's regional cuisines with recipes shared by 15 great chefs from communities in every corner of the map. I hope you will enjoy preparing these healthy meals in your home.

Michel Nischan

AN ECLECTIC MIX

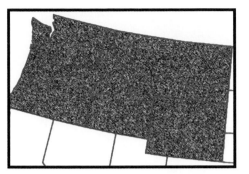

With no ties to strong ethnic traditions, the Northwest is in the process of discovering — or re-creating — its own culinary identity by mixing traditional foods with new eclectic flavors. Seafoods such as salmon, mussels, clams, crabs and oysters are staples of Northwest cooking. In the Northwest, apples, pears and berries, and vegetables such as asparagus and onions, are favorites. Coffee bars and fruit smoothies are also popular.

The vast array of healthy fruits, vegetables and seafood is one factor that may help contribute to the low incidence of type 2 diabetes in the Northwest. However, there are many factors that contribute to the incidence of this disease. Weight, family history and ethnicity are key factors in determining who will develop insulin resistance, an underlying cause of type 2 diabetes. The recipes found in this chapter — dishes like Grilled Portobello Mushrooms (page 13) and Watermelon Berry Delight (page 16) — can help you get healthier and control diabetes while still enjoying the flavors of the Northwest.

CHEF: **JACK CZARNECKI**

▶ **Copper River Salmon with Chanterelles and Red Pepper Purée**

▶ **Grilled Portobello Mushrooms**

▶ **Filet Mignon with Northwest Mushroom Sauce**

CHEF: **TOM DOUGLAS**

▶ **Watermelon Berry Delight**

▶ **Grilled Chicken Sandwich with Cucumber Yogurt**

▶ **Grilled Pacific Swordfish with Plum-Basil Relish**

CHEF ▶ JACK CZARNECKI

Named one of the top 16 chefs in the country by the James Beard Foundation, Jack Czarnecki is a certified mushroom fanatic. A critically acclaimed and published mushroom specialist, Jack's second book, *A Cook's Book of Mushrooms,* won the James Beard Award. Professionally trained in wine tasting, Jack duly credits his parents with giving him a tireless passion for food. In 1974, Jack and his wife Heidi took over his family restaurant, Joe's, the first Pennsylvania restaurant ever to earn a Mobil four-star rating. Since 1997, Jack has been winning rave reviews as chef of The Joel Palmer House in Oregon.

COPPER RIVER SALMON WITH CHANTERELLES AND RED PEPPER PURÉE

SALMON AND MUSHROOMS are typical ingredients available in this region.

For the red pepper purée:
- 2 large red peppers
- 3 tablespoons of fresh lemon juice
- 1 teaspoon of sugar
- ½ teaspoon of salt (optional)

- 2 tablespoons of olive oil
- ½ small onion, thinly sliced
- 6 ounces of fresh chanterelles or oyster mushrooms, cleaned and sliced
- ¼ teaspoon of freshly ground black pepper
- 4 6-ounce salmon filets, prepared as you like but preferably grilled

1. Preheat broiler. Place whole peppers on broiler pan and broil for 10 minutes, turning once until their skins have blackened spots and shrivels. Remove and let cool.

2. Remove the skin entirely from each pepper. Slit the peppers open and remove the stem, seeds and harder veined areas. Place the peppers in the blender and add the lemon juice, sugar and salt. Blend to a smooth purée. Place the purée in a small sauce pan and warm slightly.

3. Light the grill. Add oil to a separate medium sauce pan. Place over medium heat. Add the onion and sauté for one minute. Add the mushrooms, reduce heat, and cover. Cook until tender (about 10 minutes). Add a little water if the bottom of the pan is too dry. Add pepper.

(continued)

▶ **TABLE TALK** The James Beard Awards, often called "the Oscars of the food world," were created by the James Beard Foundation to recognize chefs for excellence and achievement. These awards are given exclusively to chefs who have served as inspirations to other food professionals.

4. Meanwhile, prepare the salmon by grilling. Cook salmon filets for 6 minutes, turning once until cooked through. To serve, place 2 tablespoons of the red pepper purée in the middle of each plate, top the purée with mushrooms and then top them both with a salmon filet.

YIELD: 4 SERVINGS **PREP TIME:** 45 MIN. **COOKING TIME:** 35 MIN.

▶**TABLE TALK: MUSHROOMS** There are over 2,500 mushroom varieties grown in the world today. Fresh mushrooms offer a multitude of distinct flavors and textures. Portobellos, shiitakes, criminis and button mushrooms are the most commonly used varieties, but the more exotic mushrooms — chanterelles, oyster mushrooms and enokis — are becoming increasingly popular.

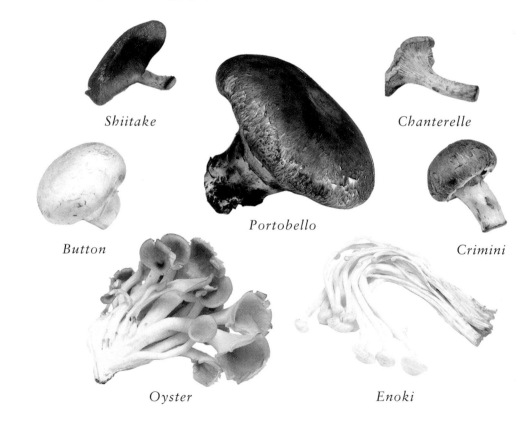

Shiitake

Chanterelle

Portobello

Button

Crimini

Oyster

Enoki

▶▶ Nutritional Information

Calories: 228 Calories from Fat: 39%

Total Fat: 10g Saturated Fat: 2g Cholesterol: 59mg Sodium: 370mg

Carbohydrate: 7g Protein: 25g Fiber: 2g

Exchanges: 3 Lean Meats & 1 Vegetable

GRILLED PORTOBELLO MUSHROOMS

THERE IS NO VEGETABLE that is meatier or more delicious than a grilled mushroom. This is the vegetarian's finest hour.

4 large portobello mushrooms
½ cup of olive oil
½ cup of red or white wine vinegar
1 tablespoon of low-sodium soy sauce
½ tablespoon of sugar
¼ cup finely chopped parsley (or ½ table-spoon of dried)
¼ cup finely chopped thyme (or ½ table-spoon of dried)

1. Separate the stems from the caps of the mushrooms. Slice each stem lengthwise.

2. In a small bowl, combine olive oil, vinegar, soy sauce, sugar, parsley and thyme and blend well with a whisk for 1 minute. Let the marinade sit for 1 hour until the dried herbs soften (not necessary if you are using fresh herbs).

3. Place the mushrooms with stems in a shallow dish or pan and pour the marinade over mushrooms. Let the mushrooms marinate for 10 minutes, but not more, turning occasionally to ensure uniform coating.

4. Light the grill. Remove the mushrooms and stems from the marinade and place over a hot grill. Grill on each side for about 2 minutes. Remove from the grill, slice, garnish with herbs and serve immediately.

YIELD: 4 SERVINGS   **PREP TIME:** 1 HOUR 20 MIN. (WITH DRIED HERBS)
COOKING TIME: 10 MIN.

▶**TABLE TALK: GRILLING** You will find recipes in this book that call for grilling as a cooking method. Grilling is a low-fat way to prepare food, but if you do not have access to a grill, use a grill pan, a cast iron skillet, or the oven broiler.

 Nutritional Information

Calories: 58 Calories from Fat: 31%

Total Fat: 2g Saturated Fat: 1g Cholesterol: 0mg Sodium: 284mg

Carbohydrate: 6g Protein: 4g Fiber: 1g

Exchanges: 1 Vegetable & ½ Fat

FILET MIGNON WITH NORTHWEST MUSHROOM SAUCE

A WONDERFUL WAY to add flavor and pizzazz to steak.

2 tablespoons of extra virgin olive oil

½ cup of onions, sliced

½ cup of water

8 ounces of fresh white mushrooms (halved) or any variety of wild mushrooms

1 teaspoon of salt (optional)

1 teaspoon of sugar

1 tablespoon of low-sodium soy sauce

½ teaspoon of dried savory

1 tablespoon of cornstarch mixed with 2 tablespoons of water

4 4-ounce portions of filet mignon

1. Light the grill. Heat oil in a medium skillet over medium-high heat. Add the onions and sauté until they become slightly browned (about 5 minutes).

2. Add the water and the mushrooms and cover the skillet. Let the mushrooms and onions simmer for ½ hour. The mushrooms will be greatly reduced in size and will be completely covered with liquid.

3. Add the salt, sugar, soy sauce and savory. Stir and let simmer for another 2 minutes. Thicken with the cornstarch mixture and keep warm.

4. Grill or oven broil the steaks to desired doneness. To serve, pour mushrooms and onions over steaks.

YIELD: 4 SERVINGS   **PREP TIME:** 20 MIN.
COOKING TIME: 45 MIN.

▶**TABLE TALK: MUSHROOMS** Mushroom varieties share common nutritional values. They are low in calories, sodium-free, fat-free and cholesterol-free, and are about one to three percent protein depending on the species.

▶▶ Nutritional Information

Calories: 315 Calories from Fat: 45%

Total Fat: 16g Saturated Fat: 5g Cholesterol: 95mg Sodium: 320mg

Carbohydrate: 8g Protein: 34g Fiber: 0g

Exchanges: 4 Lean Meats, 1 Vegetable & 1 Fat

CHEF ▶ TOM DOUGLAS

Tom Douglas has been instrumental in defining the Northwest style of cooking. Borrowing from many cultures including Asian, Alaskan, Californian and Canadian, Douglas creates unique and flavorful recipes that incorporate the finest and freshest ingredients of the Pacific Northwest. This 1994 winner of the coveted James Beard Award for Best Chef of the Northwest, currently owns three restaurants in the Seattle area — Dahlia Lounge, Palace Kitchen and Etta's Seafood. Often recognized by both the press and the public, these restaurants are considered to be Seattle's premier establishments.

Watermelon Berry Delight, recipe on page 16

WATERMELON BERRY DELIGHT

A DREAM DESSERT: delicious and few calories!

2½ pounds of watermelon

⅓ cup of cold water plus
¼ cup of cold water

4 teaspoons of unflavored
gelatin

2 tablespoons of sugar

1 vanilla bean

1 pint of either blackberries,
blueberries, raspberries
or a mixture of berries

Garnish (optional):
Fresh mint leaves

1. Smoothly line an 8-inch square glass baking dish with plastic wrap. Set aside.

2. Remove the rind from the watermelon. Cut watermelon into chunks and remove the seeds. Purée the watermelon (approximately 4 cups) in a blender. Set aside.

3. In a small, heat-proof bowl pour ⅓ cup of cold water and sprinkle gelatin over it. Allow the gelatin to soften, approximately 3 to 5 minutes.

4. Combine sugar and ¼ cup of cold water in a small saucepan over medium-high heat. Using a small paring knife, slice open the vanilla bean and scrape its seeds into the saucepan. Bring the mixture to a boil, stirring to dissolve the sugar. Pour the boiling sugar syrup over the softened gelatin and stir to dissolve the gelatin completely.

5. Add the sugar-gelatin syrup to the watermelon purée and stir to combine. Pour the watermelon mixture into the plastic-lined dish and refrigerate until firm, approximately 6 hours or overnight.

6. Remove the gelatin from the refrigerator. Place a cutting board over the baking dish and invert the gelatin onto the board. Peel off the plastic wrap. Cut the gelatin into 1-inch cubes. To serve, portion the berries into the dessert bowls. Arrange the gelatin cubes over the berries. Garnish with mint leaves.

YIELD: 6 SERVINGS   **PREP TIME:** 25 MIN.   **COOKING TIME:** 25 MIN.
COOLING TIME: 6 HOURS

Nutritional Information

Calories: 110 Calories from Fat: 0%

Total Fat: 0g Saturated Fat: 0g Cholesterol: 0mg Sodium: 9mg

Carbohydrate: 24g Protein: 3g Fiber: 2g

Exchanges: 1½ Carbs

GRILLED CHICKEN SANDWICH WITH CUCUMBER YOGURT

HERE'S A TASTY SANDWICH that's easy to make and fun to eat.

For the spice rub:

1 teaspoon of kosher salt (optional)

1 teaspoon of paprika

½ teaspoon of ground cumin

¼ teaspoon of freshly ground black pepper

¼ teaspoon of cayenne pepper

For the cucumber yogurt:

1 cup of plain low-fat yogurt

½ small cucumber, peeled, halved, seeded and diced (about 4 ounces)

2 teaspoons of fresh lemon juice

¼ teaspoon of garlic, minced

¼ teaspoon of salt (optional)

⅛ teaspoon of freshly ground black pepper

4 4-ounce boneless, skinless chicken breasts

1 tablespoon of olive oil for brushing

4 whole wheat pita breads, warmed

1 small bunch of watercress, washed and dried (discard any tough stems)

1. Light the grill. To make the spice rub: combine the salt, paprika, cumin, black pepper and cayenne pepper in small bowl. Set aside.

2. To make the cucumber yogurt: combine the yogurt, cucumber, lemon juice and garlic in a medium bowl and season with salt and pepper. Set aside.

3. Pat the chicken breasts on both sides with the spice rub. Brush the chicken and the grill lightly with olive oil and grill chicken over direct heat, with the grill covered and the vents open. When the chicken breasts are marked by the grill, flip them over and finish cooking the other side until done. The time will depend on the heat of the grill, approximately 10 to 12 minutes total.

4. Remove the chicken breasts from the grill and cut them into slices. To serve, fill the warm pitas with sliced chicken and watercress and drizzle a little cucumber yogurt into the sandwiches.

YIELD: 4 SERVINGS   **PREP TIME:** 30 MIN.
COOKING TIME: 15 MIN.

▶ Nutritional Information

Calories: 280 Calories from Fat: 22%

Total Fat: 7g Saturated Fat: 1g Cholesterol: 80mg Sodium: 347mg

Carbohydrate: 23g Protein: 30g Fiber: 2g

Exchanges: 1½ Carbs, 4 Very Lean Meats & 1 Fat

GRILLED PACIFIC SWORDFISH WITH PLUM-BASIL RELISH

FRUIT AND SEAFOOD are plentiful in the Northwest and this dish uses both.

For the spice rub:

¾ teaspoon of kosher salt (optional)

½ tablespoon of light brown sugar

1 teaspoon of paprika

¼ teaspoon of freshly ground black pepper

For the relish:

1 small bunch of fresh basil

4 medium plums, halved, pitted and thinly sliced

1 tablespoon of pine nuts

1 tablespoon of balsamic vinegar

1 tablespoon of extra virgin olive oil

¼ teaspoon of salt (optional)

⅛ teaspoon of freshly ground black pepper

4 4-ounce swordfish filets

1 tablespoon of olive oil for brushing

1. Light the grill. To make the spice rub: combine the salt, brown sugar, paprika and black pepper in a small bowl. Set aside.

2. To make the plum relish: pull the basil leaves from the stems. Reserve 4 attractive basil leaves for garnish and thinly slice the rest. Combine the sliced basil (approximately 3 tablespoons), plums, pine nuts (to toast pine nuts, swirl in a hot pan for 2–3 minutes), vinegar and olive oil in a bowl. Mix gently and season to taste with salt and pepper. Set aside.

3. Pat the spice rub on both sides of each swordfish filet. Brush the grill and the fish with a little olive oil. Grill the swordfish over direct heat, with the grill covered and the vents open. When the swordfish filets are marked by the grill, flip them over and finish cooking the other side to desired doneness. The time will depend on the heat of the grill (about 8 minutes total for medium-rare to medium). The sugar in the spice rub can burn, so watch the fish carefully and move the fish to a cooler part of the grill if needed.

4. Remove the swordfish from the grill. Divide swordfish into four portions and spoon some of the plum relish over each portion. Garnish with reserved basil leaves.

YIELD: 4 SERVINGS   PREP TIME: 30 MIN.   COOKING TIME: 15 MIN.

▶▶ Nutritional Information

Calories: 281 Calories from Fat: 38%

Total Fat: 12g Saturated Fat: <1g Cholesterol: 44mg Sodium: 464mg

Carbohydrate: 18g Protein: 26g Fiber: 2g

Exchanges: 1 Carb, 3 Lean Meats & 1 Fat

THE MELTING POT

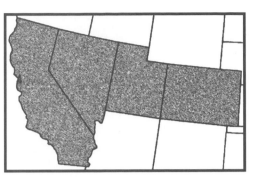

*A*merica's cutting-edge culinary frontier, the West, is a melting pot of foods from different cultures. From Chinese cuisine in San Francisco to Mexican by the border, the West offers a variety of food choices. Raw materials including fresh figs and dates, artichokes and asparagus, olive oil, raisins and garlic, are famous in this region. New age dishes, such as summer wraps and sushi in which avocado is the central ingredient, are also popular.

The West is home to many Hispanic-Americans — a population that typically has a high prevalence of type 2 diabetes. In California alone, approximately 1.3 million people are living with diabetes. The association between insulin resistance, an underlying cause of type 2 diabetes, and obesity has been recognized for many decades. Recent treatment approaches have focused on helping the body respond more effectively to its own insulin. By incorporating a glitazone such as Avandia® (rosiglitazone maleate) into a treatment plan that includes a healthy meal plan and physical activity, people can effectively manage their disease. Check with your physician about medications for diabetes management.

CHEF: MARTIN YAN

▶ Chicken with Cashews
▶ Chilled Tofu with Bean Sprouts
▶ Stir-Fried Fish with Sweet Peas

CHEF: SCOTT NEWMAN

▶ Pork Loin with Leeks
▶ Butternut Squash Risotto
▶ Alaskan Halibut with Asparagus

CHEF: EMILY LUCHETTI

▶ Cocoa Wafer Stack with Orange Whip and Raspberries

CHEFS: MARY SUE MILLIKEN & SUSAN FENIGER

▶ Chicken Tostada Salad
▶ Corn-and-Cheese-Stuffed Chiles in Rice
▶ Chipotle Black Bean Turkey Chili

CHEF ▶ MARTIN YAN

Martin Yan is a noted professor of cooking and successful cookbook author, but he is most famous as the witty and energetic star of TV's ever-popular *Yan Can Cook*, which received the prestigious James Beard Award for Best Television Cooking Show in 1994. Martin began his career as a chef's apprentice in Hong Kong and China. He practiced his craft in restaurants throughout Asia and North America, and holds a master's degree in food science from the University of California at Davis. Both skilled and light-hearted, he remains one of America's most popular food personalities.

CHICKEN with CASHEWS

AN EASY, DELICIOUS DISH that is full of flavor and very speedy to make.

For the marinade:

2 teaspoons of dry sherry

1 teaspoon of low-sodium soy sauce

1 teaspoon of cornstarch

¾ pound of boneless,
    skinless chicken breast

2 teaspoons of canola oil

2 teaspoons of ginger, minced

1 tablespoon of garlic, minced

½ onion, cut into ½-inch cubes

1 red bell pepper, cut into ½-inch cubes

1 small zucchini, cut into ½-inch cubes

½ cup of low-sodium chicken broth

½ teaspoon of sesame oil

1 teaspoon of cornstarch dissolved in
    2 teaspoons of water

¼ cup of roasted cashews
    (may substitute walnuts)

1. Combine sherry, soy sauce and cornstarch in a medium bowl. Cut chicken into ½-inch cubes. Add chicken to marinade and stir to coat. Let stand for 10 minutes.

2. Place a wok over high heat until hot. Add cooking oil, swirling to coat sides. Add ginger and garlic and cook until fragrant, about 10 seconds. Add chicken and stir-fry for 2 minutes.

3. Add onion, bell pepper, zucchini and chicken broth. Cover and cook until vegetables are tender-crisp, about 2 minutes. Add sesame oil. Mix well.

4. Add cornstarch solution to pan and cook, stirring, until sauce boils and thickens. Add nuts and mix well. May be served with steamed rice.

YIELD: 4 SERVINGS   **PREP TIME:** 30 MIN.
COOKING TIME: 20 MIN.

▶ Nutritional Information

Calories: 248   Calories from Fat: 47%

Total Fat: 13g   Saturated Fat: 2g   Cholesterol: 59.5mg   Sodium: 181mg

Carbohydrate: 9g   Protein: 22g   Fiber: 2g

Exchanges: ½ Carb, 3 Lean Meats & 1 Fat

CHILLED TOFU WITH BEAN SPROUTS

EXOTIC AND MELLOW with sesame flavor and interesting texture.

½ pound of bean sprouts

1 teaspoon of sesame seeds

For the dressing:

3 tablespoons of rice vinegar

1 tablespoon of low-sodium soy sauce

1 tablespoon of canola or olive oil

1 teaspoon of sesame oil

1 teaspoon of honey

1 package (16 oz.) of soft tofu, drained

Garnish (optional):

2 tablespoons of roasted walnuts or almonds, chopped

1. Bring a pot of water to a boil. Add bean sprouts and boil for 1 minute. Drain bean sprouts, rinse with cold water, and drain again. Place on a serving plate, cover and refrigerate until chilled.

2. Place sesame seeds in a small frying pan over medium heat. Toast seeds by shaking the pan frequently, until seeds are lightly browned, 3–4 minutes. Immediately remove from pan to cool.

3. Combine rice vinegar, soy sauce, canola or olive oil, sesame oil and honey in a small bowl. Set aside. Cut tofu into ½-inch cubes. To serve, place tofu over chilled bean sprouts, drizzle dressing over tofu and garnish with sesame seeds and nuts.

YIELD: 4 SERVINGS   **PREP TIME:** 20 MIN.

COOKING TIME: 20 MIN.

▶ **TABLE TALK: FATS** Fats are considered the most concentrated source of calories. Your daily share of calories should be 30% or less, with only 10% from saturated fat.

▶▶ Nutritional Information

Calories: 132 Calories from Fat: 37%

Total Fat: 7g Saturated Fat: 1g Cholesterol: 0mg Sodium: 164mg

Carbohydrate: 7g Protein: 7g Fiber: 1g

Exchanges: ½ Carb, 1 Very Lean Meat & 1 Fat

STIR-FRIED FISH WITH SWEET PEAS

THIS IS A COMPLETE, quick meal in itself when served over steamed rice.

1 pound of rock cod filets

For the marinade:

1 egg white

⅛ teaspoon of garlic, minced

⅛ teaspoon of salt (optional)

a pinch of freshly ground black
pepper

3 teaspoons of canola oil

1 cup of fresh or frozen
sweet peas

4 slices of ginger

a dash of sesame oil

a dash of dry white cooking wine

1 teaspoon of cornstarch
dissolved in ½ cup of water

Garnish (optional):

Carrots, straw mushrooms and
yellow chives, thinly sliced
into matchstick strips

1. Slice or butterfly each fish filet.

2. Combine egg white, garlic, salt and pepper in a medium bowl. Add fish and stir to coat each piece of fish. Let stand for 15 minutes.

3. Heat a non-stick pan with 2 teaspoons of oil. Swirl to coat sides of pan. Pan-fry fish until almost cooked. Remove from pan.

4. Return the pan to high heat, and add the remaining 1 teaspoon of oil. Add sweet peas and ginger. Stir-fry for 1 minute. Return fish to pan, and add sesame oil and cooking wine.

5. Add cornstarch solution and cook, stirring until gravy thickens. Once gravy thickens, remove from pan. Serve with a garnish of carrots, straw mushrooms and yellow chives.

YIELD: 4 SERVINGS   PREP TIME: 20 MIN.

COOKING TIME: 25 MIN.

▶TABLE TALK: COOKING WITH A WOK For healthy cooking, think about purchasing a wok. This round, deep Chinese-style pan is specifically made for stir-frying. The curved bottom of the wok makes it possible to cook with very little oil.

Nutritional
Information

Calories: 168 Calories from Fat: 11%

Total Fat: 2g Saturated Fat: <1g Cholesterol: 49mg Sodium: 352mg

Carbohydrate: 5g Protein: 25g Fiber: 1g

Exchanges: 3 Very Lean Meats & 1 Vegetable

CHEF ▶ SCOTT NEWMAN

Scott Newman once dreamed of becoming a Broadway star. While studying to be an actor and performing on stage, he supported himself by cooking at various restaurants throughout New York City. He soon fell in love with food, and the rest is restaurant history. In 1988, the young cook apprenticed at Masa's in San Francisco, where he was inspired by the world-renowned chef Julian Serrano. Next, he worked for three years as the Sous-Chef at Patina in Los Angeles. Today, Scott is the celebrated Executive Chef at Rubicon, one of San Francisco's finest restaurants.

PORK LOIN WITH LEEKS

A SUCCULENT roast with lots of flavor.

1 carrot, diced finely

2 stalks of celery, diced finely

1 yellow onion, diced finely

2 tablespoons water

4 heads of leek, white part only

2 tablespoons of olive oil

2 russet potatoes (1 pound), peeled and diced

2 8-ounce pork tenderloins

1 cup of low-sodium chicken broth

½ bunch of parsley, de-stemmed and chopped

Garnish (optional):

1 bunch of chives, chopped

1. Preheat the oven to 375 degrees. In a large skillet, sauté the carrot, celery and onion with the water until soft, about 5 minutes. Remove from the skillet. Set aside.

2. Cut leeks into half moons and sauté in oil for 3 minutes. Set aside.

3. Cook potatoes in boiling water until just cooked through. Set aside.

4. Place pork in a roasting pan. Roast in oven until cooked medium-rare to medium, about 30 minutes. Let the meat rest for about 10 minutes before slicing.

5. In a large pot over medium heat, combine the leeks, potatoes and broth. Keep covered until the leeks are tender, about 10 minutes. Stir in the chopped parsley.

CELEBRITY CHEFS ACROSS AMERICA

▶▶ Nutritional Information

24

Calories: 325 Calories from Fat: 27%

Total Fat: 10g Saturated Fat: 5g Cholesterol: 55mg Sodium: 321mg

Carbohydrate: 35g Protein: 24g Fiber: 5g

Exchanges: 2 Carbs, 2 Medium-Fat Meats & 1 Vegetable

6. With a slotted spoon, remove the leeks and potatoes from the broth and divide them among the four plates. Add the carrot, celery and onion mixture to the broth and simmer for 5 minutes or until vegetables are tender.

7. To serve, divide the meat into four equal portions and lay it over the potatoes and leeks. Top with the vegetable sauce. Sprinkle each serving with chopped chives.

YIELD: 4 SERVINGS   **PREP TIME:** 45 MIN.   **COOKING TIME:** I HOUR 30 MIN.

BUTTERNUT SQUASH RISOTTO

EVERYONE LOVES A SMOOTH, luscious risotto.

½ large or 1 small butternut
squash (1¼ pounds)

2 tablespoons of olive oil

2 tablespoons of water

For the risotto:

½ onion, diced

1 cup of aborio rice

¼ cup of dry white wine

3 cups of low-sodium
chicken broth, heated

¼ cup of grated parmesan
cheese

Garnish (optional):

1 tablespoon of parsley,
finely chopped

1 teaspoon of fresh thyme,
finely chopped

1. Preheat the oven to 350 degrees. Cut the butternut squash in half and remove seeds. Cut ½ of the squash into a ¼-inch dice. Take the remaining squash, coat with 1 tablespoon of olive oil and roast in the oven until soft, about 35 minutes. Remove the skin from the roasted squash and purée the flesh in a blender with 1 teaspoon of olive oil and 2 tablespoons of water. Set purée aside.

2. Meanwhile, fill a small saucepan ¾ full with water and bring to a boil. Add the diced squash and cook for 3–4 minutes until just cooked through. Rinse with cold water when done to stop the cooking process. Set aside.

3. To make the risotto: sauté the diced onion over medium-low heat with 2 teaspoons of olive oil in a heavy-bottomed, medium-sized pot, about 3–4 minutes. When the onion is soft but has not browned, add the rice and stir for 2 minutes to toast the rice.

4. Stirring continuously, add the white wine and allow it to slowly evaporate. Add small amounts of hot chicken broth, stirring constantly so the rice slowly absorbs the broth without sticking to the pot. Keep adding broth until the rice is cooked, about 20 minutes.

5. Add the squash purée and cheese and stir. To serve, top with diced squash, parsley and thyme. Serve immediately.

YIELD: 4 SERVINGS   PREP TIME: 45 MIN.   COOKING TIME: 1 HOUR 15 MIN.

 Nutritional
Information

Calories: 296 Calories from Fat: 24%

Total Fat: 8g Saturated Fat: 2g Cholesterol: 4mg Sodium: 307mg

Carbohydrate: 44g Protein: 7g Fiber: 1g

Exchanges: 3 Carbs & 1½ Fats

ALASKAN HALIBUT WITH ASPARAGUS

ONE OF AMERICA'S GREATEST fish given a royal treatment.

For the asparagus:

2 bunches of large asparagus (approximately 20 pieces), peeled

1 cup of flour

3 eggs, beaten or ¾ cup of egg substitute

1 cup of dried bread crumbs

2 tablespoons & 2 teaspoons of butter or margarine

4 5-ounce Alaskan halibut filets

1¼ pounds of wild mushrooms (cepes, morels or chanterelles)

2 tablespoons of Madeira wine

4 ounces (about 10 tablespoons) of low-sodium chicken broth

1 tablespoon of parsley, chopped

1½ teaspoons of thyme, chopped

Garnish (optional):

1 cup of Port wine cooked down to ⅛ cup (over low heat)

1. Cook asparagus in a large pot of boiling water for 2 minutes. Remove from pot and cool under cold water. Cut ends to make all tips even.

2. Dip asparagus in flour, then eggs, then bread crumbs and sauté in 1 tablespoon of butter or margarine until golden brown on both sides. Set aside.

3. Heat 1 teaspoon of butter or margarine in a non-stick pan. Add halibut and cook over medium heat for 5 minutes, turning until cooked through. Set aside.

4. Sauté mushrooms in 1 tablespoon of butter or margarine until browned. Pour Madeira wine and chicken broth into pan and reduce by half. Add the chopped parsley and thyme. Add 1 teaspoon of butter or margarine. To serve, divide asparagus into four portions, spoon mushrooms over asparagus, place the sautéed halibut on top and drizzle Port wine to garnish.

YIELD: 4 SERVINGS   **PREP TIME:** 40 MIN.
COOKING TIME: 40 MIN.

▶▶ Nutritional Information

Calories: 416 Calories from Fat: 30%

Total Fat: 14g Saturated Fat: 6g Cholesterol: 135mg Sodium: 397mg

Carbohydrate: 34g Protein: 36g Fiber: 5g

Exchanges: 2 Carbs, 4 Lean Meats & ½ Fat

CHEF ▶ EMILY LUCHETTI

Emily Luchetti works diligently to create desserts that are "emotionally fulfilling," simple to prepare and wonderful to eat. Currently the Executive Pastry Chef at the renowned Farallon restaurant in San Francisco, Emily has been bestowed with many accolades, including several nominations for a coveted James Beard culinary award. Motivated by her twin brother, who lives with diabetes, Emily has committed her great talents to providing delicious, low-fat recipes that you can easily prepare at home. The extraordinary recipes crafted by this master pastry chef are often featured in national magazines and on television.

COCOA WAFER STACK WITH ORANGE WHIP AND RASPBERRIES

FAST AND EASY, this dramatic looking dessert will be appreciated, especially by the kids (see photo on cover).

½ cup of light non-dairy whipped topping

½ teaspoon of grated orange zest

16 chocolate wafers

4 ounces of raspberries

1. In a small bowl, gently fold together the light whipped topping and the orange zest.

2. Place one chocolate wafer on each of four plates. Spoon one tablespoon of the orange topping onto the center of each wafer. Place 4 raspberries on the wafer, surrounding the topping.

3. Place a second chocolate wafer on top and again spoon one tablespoon of the orange light whipped topping onto the center and surround with four raspberries. Repeat this layering with a third chocolate wafer. Finally, top with the fourth cookie.

4. If desired, these stacks can be made ahead and refrigerated. As the stacks sit, the wafers become softer. Transfer carefully onto plates.

YIELD: 4 SERVINGS   PREP TIME: 10 MIN.

Nutritional Information

Calories: 173 Calories from Fat: 31%

Total Fat: 6g Saturated Fat: 3g Cholesterol: 2mg Sodium 184mg

Carbohydrate: 24g Protein: 1.6g Fiber: 2g

Exchanges: 1½ Carbs & 1 Fat

CHEF ▶ Mary Sue Milliken & Susan Feniger

Mary Sue Milliken and Susan Feniger are two of America's most beloved chefs. Making their mark with home cooking from all over the world, the pair are chefs/owners of the critically acclaimed Border Grill Mexican restaurants in Santa Monica and Las Vegas, as well as Ciudad in Downtown Los Angeles, serving seductive foods from all over the Latin world. Veterans of 296 episodes of the popular *Too Hot Tamales* series with Food Network, the duo has now signed for a new series with PBS. Their recent cookbook, *Mexican Cooking for Dummies*, is their fifth.

CHICKEN TOSTADA SALAD

Lively and spicy with crisp textures and lots of flavor.

¾ pound of cooked, shredded chicken breast (about 2 cups)

1 small red onion, diced

½ cup fresh cilantro leaves, chopped

1 small or ½ large head of romaine lettuce

1 medium tomato, cored, seeded and diced

¼ cup (1 ounce) of grated anejo or pepper jack cheese

4 ounces of baked, unsalted tortilla chips

1 cup of canned, fat-free refried black beans

For the dressing:

2 tablespoons of red wine vinegar

3 tablespoons of olive oil

Salt & pepper to taste (optional)

3 tablespoons of fat-free sour cream

1. Combine the chicken, onion and cilantro in a medium bowl.

2. In another bowl, combine the lettuce, tomato, cheese and 3 ounces of tortilla chips.

3. In a small pot, heat the beans over low heat, stirring often to prevent sticking. Add some water if the beans are dry (about 3 tablespoons).

4. To make the dressing, combine red wine vinegar, olive oil, salt and pepper in a small jar or bottle. Cover and shake vigorously to combine, or whisk the ingredients together.

(continued)

 Nutritional Information

Calories: 465 Calories from Fat: 33%

Total Fat: 17g Saturated Fat: 2g Cholesterol: 80mg Sodium: 457mg

Carbohydrate: 45g Protein: 37g Fiber: 9 g

Exchanges: 3 Carbs, 4 Lean Meats & 1 Fat

5. To serve, pour half of the dressing on the reserved chicken mixture to coat generously, and toss well. Pour the remaining half of the dressing on the lettuce mixture, toss well, and divide on four plates. Top with chicken mixture, ¼ cup of refried beans and ¾ tablespoon of sour cream. Garnish with 1 ounce of baked tortilla chips.

YIELD: 4 SERVINGS **PREP TIME**: 25 MIN. **COOKING TIME**: 15 MIN.

CORN-and-CHEESE-STUFFED CHILES in rice

THIS MEXICAN SPECIALTY is a delightful side dish or main course.

1 tablespoon of canola oil

1 medium yellow onion, chopped

2 cloves of garlic, peeled and minced

2 cups of fresh corn kernels (about 4 ears) or 2 10-ounce packages of frozen corn

1 teaspoon of freshly ground black pepper

½ cup (4 ounces) of grated low-fat monterey jack cheese

6 large poblano chiles, roasted and peeled

2 cups of cooked white rice

½ cup of low-fat sour cream

½ cup of salsa

½ cup (2 ounces) of grated anejo or pepper jack cheese

1. Preheat the oven to 350 degrees. Heat the oil in a medium saucepan over medium heat. Sauté the onion for about 5 minutes until transparent (clear). Add the garlic and cook for 1 minute longer. Add the corn and pepper, and sauté until tender, about 2½ minutes. Transfer to a bowl and let cool. Stir in the monterey jack cheese and set aside.

2. Roast the chiles under the broiler or directly on the stovetop until charred on all sides. Place in a sealed plastic bag to sweat for about 20 minutes. Gently rub off the skins. Carefully slit the chiles lengthwise, removing the seeds and veins, leaving the stems and tops intact if possible. Stuff the chiles with the reserved corn mixture.

3. Spray a 13-by 9-inch glass baking dish with non-stick cooking spray. Arrange the rice in the dish and nestle the chiles in the rice in a single layer.

4. Combine sour cream and salsa and pour on top of rice. Sprinkle with pepper jack cheese and transfer to oven. Bake for about 25 minutes until heated through. Serve hot.

YIELD: 6 SERVINGS PREP TIME: I HOUR AND 25 MIN. (INCLUDING PREPARATION OF RICE AND ROASTING OF CHILES) COOKING TIME: 35 MIN.

 Nutritional Information

Calories: 267 Calories from Fat: 41%

Total Fat: 12 g Saturated Fat: 3 g Cholesterol: 30mg Sodium: 324mg

Carbohydrate: 29 g Protein: 11.5 g Fiber: <1 g

Exchanges: 2 Carbs, 1 Medium-Fat Meat & 1 Fat

CHIPOTLE BLACK BEAN TURKEY CHILI

THIS IS A FLAVORFUL AND DELICIOUS one-dish lunch that makes great leftovers.

1 cup of dry black beans

4 cups of water

1 arbol or jalapeño chile

2 small bay leaves

1 tablespoon of vegetable oil

½ pound of coarsely ground turkey, white meat

½ large yellow onion, diced

¼ teaspoon of salt (optional)

¼ teaspoon of freshly ground black pepper

2 cloves of garlic, peeled and minced

1 green bell pepper, stemmed, seeded and diced

½ tablespoon of chili powder

½ tablespoon of ground cumin

2 canned chipotle chiles, stemmed and minced

1 cup of low-sodium chicken broth

2 tablespoons of low-fat or fat-free sour cream

1. Place the beans in a large pot with the water, the arbol or jalapeño chile and bay leaves. Bring to a boil. Reduce to a simmer and cover. Cook until tender, about 1 hour. Remove and discard the chile and bay leaves. Do not drain the beans.

2. Heat the vegetable oil in a large heavy pot over medium-high heat. Cook the turkey, stirring often and breaking up with a spoon, until evenly browned.

3. Add the onion, salt and pepper and sauté over moderate heat, stirring occasionally, until lightly golden, about 10 minutes.

4. Stir in the garlic, green pepper, chili powder, cumin and chipotles. Cook, stirring frequently, for 3 minutes, or until aromas are released.

5. Stir in the black beans with their liquid and the chicken broth. Cook uncovered for 40 minutes or until the flavors have blended and the chili has thickened. To serve, divide into four bowls and add 1½ teaspoons of sour cream on top of each.

YIELD: 4 SERVINGS **PREP TIME:** 10 MIN. **COOKING TIME:** 2 HOURS

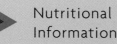 Nutritional Information

Calories: 402 Calories from Fat: 33%

Total Fat: 15g Saturated Fat: 6g Cholesterol: 66mg Sodium: 391mg

Carbohydrate: 38g Protein: 29g Fiber: 8g

Exchanges: 2½ Carbs, 3 Lean Meats & 1 Fat

CELEBRITY CHEFS ACROSS AMERICA

DISTINCTIVE CUISINE

Known for its dramatic colors, bold flavors and zesty seasonings, the Southwest has one of the most distinctive regional cuisines in America. Spanish immigrants were the first to begin cultivating and adding chile peppers to Southwestern cooking, and the Native Americans continue to influence this region with the widespread use of beans and corn. American cowboys left their mark on Southwestern cuisine with the original cookout of barbecued chicken and ribs. Unusual ingredients such as cactus, salsa and tomatillos also are hallmarks of this region's cuisine.

Southwestern recipes, such as Pueblo Squash Stew (page 40) and Roasted Carrot Soup (page 44), can be prepared without compromising the distinctive regional taste — a common concern for people with type 2 diabetes who need to be consistent with their meal plan. In this chapter, you will find recipes that will help guide you in creating healthy, exciting meals with a Southwestern flair. It's important to remember that in order to control type 2 diabetes, it's critical to eat a proper diet and exercise regularly. Some people may need to add medication to their daily regimen. Talk to your physician about treatment options such as glitazones, a class of drugs that directly target insulin resistance, an underlying cause of type 2 diabetes.

CHEF: RICHARD CHAMBERLAIN
- ▶ Southwest Roast Turkey
- ▶ Southwest Grilled Potatoes
- ▶ Filet Mignon with Spicy Steak Rub
- ▶ Tuna Steak with Sweet Pepper Aioli
- ▶ Turkey and Egg Enchiladas with Chipotle Sauce
- ▶ Pueblo Squash Stew
- ▶ Navajo Green Chili Stew

CHEF: MARK TARBELL
- ▶ Lime-Marinated Shrimp
- ▶ Roasted Carrot Soup with Roma Tomatoes
- ▶ Grilled Salmon Provencal

CHEF: EMILY LUCHETTI
- ▶ Coffee Amaretto Parfait

SOUTHWEST

CHEF ► RICHARD CHAMBERLAIN

Known for mastering and refining Southwestern regional cuisine, Richard Chamberlain is an innovator, particularly in the area of unique cooking with steaks and fish. In the late 1980's, Richard secured a spot as one of *Food & Wine* magazine's Rising Stars to Watch. In 1993 his restaurant, Chamberlain's Steak and Chop House, located just outside Dallas, was named one of the country's top new restaurants by *Bon Appétit* magazine. In 1998, *Gourmet* rated Chamberlain's as one of America's Top Tables, and in both 1999 and 2000 Chamberlain's was voted one of America's Top Restaurants by the *Zagat Survey*.

SOUTHWEST ROAST TURKEY

A FLAVORFUL MAIN COURSE and sandwich meat for the rest of the week.

For marinade:

⅓ cup of lime juice

½ cup of chili powder

½ cup of dark brown sugar

2 tablespoons of olive oil

2 cups of water

½ tablespoon of salt (optional)

1 whole turkey breast (approximately 3–4 pounds)

1. To prepare the marinade, combine lime juice, chili powder, sugar, olive oil, water and salt in a saucepan and bring to a boil over medium-high heat. Remove from the saucepan and chill.

2. Place the turkey in a large bowl. Pour in the marinade mixture. Refrigerate for at least 4 hours.

3. To cook the turkey, preheat the oven to 375 degrees. Remove the turkey breast from the bowl and reserve the marinade. Place the turkey breast, skin side up, on a roasting pan. Cook for 35–40 minutes or until the internal temperature is 160 degrees. Baste the turkey occasionally with reserved marinade.

4. Remove turkey from oven and allow it to rest for 8–10 minutes. Slice and serve. Use remaining turkey to make salads and sandwiches for your family.

YIELD: 12 SERVINGS   PREP TIME: 4 HOURS 30 MIN. (INCLUDING MARINATING TIME)
COOKING TIME: 1 HOUR

Nutritional Information

Calories: 173 Calories from Fat: 26%

Total Fat: 5g Saturated Fat: 1g Cholesterol: 52mg Sodium: 375mg

Carbohydrate: 8g Protein: 23g Fiber: 0g

Exchanges: ½ Carb, 3 Very Lean Meats & ½ Fat

SOUTHWEST GRILLED POTATOES

THESE SPICED POTATOES are so delicious, everyone will beg for more.

1½ pounds of small new red potatoes, unpeeled and well-scrubbed, cut in half if large

¼ teaspoon of salt (optional)

1 tablespoon of olive oil

1 tablespoon of chili powder

1 tablespoon of freshly grated parmesan cheese

2 teaspoons of cilantro pesto (may substitute basil pesto)

¼ teaspoon of freshly ground black pepper

1. Light the grill.

2. Fill a large pot ¾ full with water and bring to a boil over high heat. Add the potatoes and salt, and cook for 10 minutes. Drain well in a colander and set aside to cool.

3. In a large bowl, combine oil and chili powder, and toss potatoes. Place potatoes on hot grill, turning occasionally until browned on all sides.

4. In a separate mixing bowl, toss browned potatoes with parmesan cheese, pesto and fresh pepper. Serve.

YIELD: 4 SERVINGS   **PREP TIME:** 25 MIN.
COOKING TIME: 45 MIN.

▶ **TABLE TALK: POTATOES** The potato is one of the most versatile vegetables in the world. Potatoes make a great accompaniment to any meat course because they easily absorb the flavors of sauces and meat juices. Red potatoes are often preferred because potatoes with their skins on are more flavorful and more nutritious than peeled potatoes.

 Nutritional Information

Calories: 178 Calories from Fat: 25%

Total Fat: 5g Saturated Fat: <1g Cholesterol: 2mg Sodium: 66mg

Carbohydrate: 28g Protein: 5g Fiber: 3g

Exchanges: 2 Carbs & 1 Fat

FILET MIGNON with SPICY STEAK RUB

A STEAK COOKED TO PERFECTION with regional spices.

For steak rub:

4 tablespoons of Hungarian paprika

3 tablespoons of chili powder

2 teaspoons of cayenne pepper

2 teaspoons of dried oregano

¾ teaspoon of salt (optional)

1 tablespoon of freshly ground black pepper

2 teaspoons of ground sage

2 tablespoons of dried mustard

1½ tablespoons of cumin

1 tablespoon of dark brown sugar

1 tablespoon of granulated sugar

4 tablespoons of garlic powder

4 6-ounce filet mignons (may substitute London broil, New York steak, or other cut of beef)

1. In a small bowl, combine paprika, chili powder, cayenne pepper, oregano, salt, black pepper, sage, mustard, cumin, brown sugar, granulated sugar and garlic powder. Store in a tightly sealed container.

2. The night before you plan to cook this dish, sprinkle the stored mixture over the meat and let it marinate for several hours or overnight.

3. Light the grill. Grill steaks over high heat to desired doneness or cook 3 minutes per side for medium.

YIELD: 4 SERVINGS   PREP TIME: 6 HOURS (INCLUDING MARINATING TIME)

COOKING TIME: 10 MIN.

▶TABLE TALK: FILET MIGNON Filet mignon is a lean, boneless cut of beef which comes from the small end of the tenderloin. Calorie-for-calorie, beef has more nutrients than most other foods, including iron, zinc, phosphorous and B-complex vitamins. One serving of lean beef contains just 6.4 grams of fat, on average. A suggested serving is a portion the size of a deck of cards.

Nutritional Information

Calories: 328 Calories from Fat: 32%

Total Fat: 12g Saturated Fat: 3.5g Cholesterol: 64mg Sodium: 532mg

Carbohydrate: 21.5g Protein: 31.5g Fiber: 0g

Exchanges: 1½ Carbs & 4 Lean Meats

TUNA STEAK WITH SWEET PEPPER AIOLI

A QUICK AND DELICIOUS WAY to prepare fish with a Southwestern taste.

For sweet pepper aioli sauce:

2 red bell peppers, roasted, peeled & seeded

2 cloves of garlic, chopped finely

3 tablespoons of fresh squeezed lime juice

½ cup of low-fat mayonnaise

1 pinch of cayenne pepper

1 teaspoon of chili powder

1 teaspoon of honey

2 tablespoons of olive oil

2 tablespoons of freshly ground black pepper

4 6-ounce tuna steaks

¼ teaspoon of salt (optional)

1. Preheat the broiler.

2. Prepare the sweet pepper aioli sauce by combining peppers, garlic, lime juice, mayonnaise, cayenne pepper, chili powder and honey in a food processor and mixing on high speed for 30 seconds or with a hand blender for 1-2 minutes until blended well. Set aside.

3. Pour the olive oil onto a plate. Place the pepper on another plate. Dip the tuna in the oil and then press some pepper onto both sides of each steak. Sprinkle with salt if desired.

4. Place the steaks on a broiler pan and broil, turning once, until cooked to desired degree of doneness, 2-3 minutes on each side for medium-rare. Serve with sweet pepper aioli sauce for dipping on the side — approximately 2 tablespoons per serving.

YIELD: 4 SERVINGS   **PREP TIME:** 20 MIN.

COOKING TIME: 30 MIN. (INCLUDING TIME TO ROAST PEPPERS)

▶**TABLE TALK: AIOLI** Sweet pepper aioli is the perfect low-fat accompaniment to fish and potato dishes. Aioli can be made simply by mixing low-fat mayonnaise with garlic or by adding some hot spices to give it a Southwestern flair. Many versions of aioli exist these days and make wonderful sauces and sandwich spreads.

 Nutritional Information

Calories: 275 Calories from Fat: 42%

Total Fat: 13g Saturated Fat: 2g Cholesterol: 64mg Sodium: 320mg

Carbohydrate: 9g Protein: 30g Fiber: 0g

Exchanges: ½ Carb & 4 Lean Meats

TURKEY AND EGG ENCHILADAS WITH CHIPOTLE SAUCE

THIS TAKES A LITTLE TIME, but the result is amazing. No one will believe you made it.

½ pound of boneless turkey breast (about 8 ounces)

1 clove of garlic

4 tomatoes, coarsely chopped

1 medium onion, cut into quarters

1 tablespoon of canned chipotle chile pepper in red adobe sauce

1 whole egg and 4 egg whites, whisked

1 tablespoon of vegetable oil

4 fat-free flour or whole wheat tortillas

2 tablespoons of queso fresco or feta cheese, crumbled

1. Preheat oven to 450 degrees. Spray baking dish with non-stick spray. Set aside.

2. Place the turkey in a saucepan with enough water to cover it. Bring to a boil and reduce the heat to low. Cover and simmer until tender, about 15-20 minutes. Drain well and let cool. Using your fingers or 2 forks, shred the meat and set aside.

3. Heat a dry, heavy frying pan or griddle over medium heat. Add the garlic, tomatoes and onion to the pan or griddle and roast, turning often, until well-charred, about 3 minutes for the garlic, 4 minutes for the tomatoes, and 5 minutes for the onions.

4. In a blender or food processor fitted with the metal blade, combine the tomatoes, garlic, onion and chile. Purée until smooth. In a non-stick pan over high heat, add the purée and cook, stirring, until thickened, about 5 minutes. Set aside.

5. In a non-stick pan, cook eggs and egg whites in the oil until soft scrambled.

6. Dip each tortilla into the tomato sauce. Top with some of the eggs and turkey then roll it into a cylinder. Place seam side down in the baking dish. When all of the enchiladas have been formed, pour the remaining sauce over the top and sprinkle with the cheese. Bake until the cheese melts, about 10 minutes. Serve immediately.

YIELD: 4 SERVINGS   **PREP TIME:** 1 HOUR 15 MIN.   **COOKING TIME:** 1 HOUR 15 MIN.

 Nutritional Information

Calories: 263 Calories from Fat: 27%

Fat: 8g Saturated Fat: 2g Cholesterol: 97mg Sodium: 371mg

Carbohydrate: 22g Protein: 27g Fiber: 11g

Exchanges: 1½ Carbs & 3 Lean Meats

PUEBLO SQUASH STEW

HERE'S A QUICK AND EASY Native American entrée.

2 teaspoons of corn oil

1 medium-sized onion, diced

2 teaspoons of garlic, minced

½ cup of low-sodium chicken broth

¾ cup of corn kernels cut off cob (or substitute ¾ cup of frozen corn kernels)

2 cups of yellow squash, diced

2 tomatoes, halved and sliced

2 tablespoons of queso fresco or feta cheese, crumbled

¼ teaspoon of salt (optional)

⅛ teaspoon of freshly ground black pepper

1. In a cast iron skillet over medium-high heat, add oil and onion. Sauté onion for approximately 3 minutes.

2. Add garlic and continue cooking for 1 minute.

3. Add chicken broth, corn, and squash. Reduce heat to medium. Simmer until squash is just soft.

4. Add tomatoes and cook until tomatoes are warm but not mushy. Sprinkle with cheese and season lightly with salt and pepper. Serve.

YIELD: 4 SERVINGS   **PREP TIME:** 20 MIN.
COOKING TIME: 30 MIN.

 Nutritional Information

Calories: 101 Calories from Fat: 27%

Total Fat: 3g Saturated Fat: <1g Cholesterol: 2mg Sodium: 293mg

Carbohydrate: 15g Protein: 4g Fiber: 3g

Exchanges: 1 Carb & ½ Fat

NAVAJO GREEN CHILI STEW

A TRADITIONAL NATIVE AMERICAN stew loaded with flavor and nutrients.

8 Anaheim chiles, roasted, peeled, seeded and diced

1 tablespoon of corn oil

1 pound of lean pork stew meat (1-inch cubes)

1 cup of yellow onion, diced

6 cloves of garlic, chopped

2 cups of low-sodium chicken broth

1 teaspoon of dry oregano or 1 tablespoon of fresh oregano

¼ teaspoon of salt (optional)

1 cup of fresh cilantro

1. Roast the chiles under the broiler or directly on the stovetop until charred on all sides. Place in a sealed plastic bag to sweat for about 20 minutes. Gently rub off the skins. Carefully slit the chiles lengthwise, removing seeds and veins. Dice chiles and reserve.

2. In a cast iron skillet over medium-high heat, add oil and pork. Brown well.

3. Add onion and garlic and continue cooking, stirring for 3 minutes. Add 1½ cups of the chicken broth and bring to a simmer. Loosen the browned bits in the skillet with a wooden spoon.

4. Add oregano, chiles and salt. Reduce the heat to medium-low and simmer for 1 hour.

5. Separately, purée the cilantro with the remaining ½ cup of chicken broth. Add the cilantro purée to the stew. Cook for an additional 10 minutes and serve.

YIELD: 4 SERVINGS   PREP TIME: 30 MIN.   COOKING TIME: 2 HOURS (INCLUDING TIME TO ROAST THE CHILES)

▶TABLE TALK: CULTURES AND MEAL PLANNING To develop a meal plan that fits your family's food tastes, cultural customs and lifestyle, while meeting your health goals, follow these simple rules:

- Eat a variety of foods
- Eat more fruits and vegetables
- Cut down on portion size
- Eat less fat
- Know your health goals

Nutritional Information

Calories: 268 Calories from Fat: 33%

Total Fat: 10g Saturated Fat: 2.4g Cholesterol: 62mg Sodium: 404mg

Carbohydrate: 19g Protein: 29g Fiber: 2.5g

Exchanges: 1 Carb & 4 Lean Meats

CHEF ▶ MARK TARBELL

The culinary mastery of Chef Mark Tarbell has been enjoyed by many, as he has prepared feasts for the Dalai Lama of Tibet, as well as at the James Beard House in New York. In 1996, he was named one of the Chefs to Keep Your Eye On by *Esquire* magazine. In 1999, he was inducted into the Scottsdale Culinary Institute's Hall of Fame. Mark has also been featured on television's *Ready, Set, Cook* and *Cooking Live* with Sara Moulton. With an energetic, straightforward style of cooking, Mark's two restaurants, Tarbell's and Barmouche, are testaments to his pioneering role in the world of distinctive cuisine.

LIME-MARINATED SHRIMP

TANGY, FRESH AND LIVELY, this is the perfect warm weather dish.

1 pound of shrimp (25/30 per pound), peeled and de-veined, leaving tails on

For the marinade:

1 shallot, minced

2 cloves of garlic, minced

2 serrano chiles, stemmed, seeded and chopped finely

4 scallions, thinly sliced

½ cup of fresh cilantro, chopped

½ cup of parsley, chopped

2 tablespoons of honey

½ cup of water

⅛ teaspoon of freshly ground black pepper

1 cup of fresh lime juice

¼ teaspoon of salt (optional)

½ cup of olive oil

1. Place cleaned shrimp in a small bowl and refrigerate.

2. Combine shallot, garlic, chiles, scallions, cilantro, parsley, honey, water and pepper in a medium mixing bowl. In a medium bowl, combine lime juice and salt, and slowly whisk in olive oil. Add lime-oil mixture to other ingredients. Pour marinade over shrimp and refrigerate for 1 hour before grilling.

3. Light the grill.

4. Remove the shrimp from the refrigerator and drain for five minutes before grilling. Thread 5-6 shrimp on a wooden or metal kebob stick. Make sure the grill is clean and hot. Place shrimp on grill and cook approximately 2–3 minutes on each side. Serve immediately.

YIELD: 4 SERVINGS   **PREP TIME:** I HOUR 15 MIN. (INCLUDING MARINATING TIME)
COOKING TIME: 10 MIN.

► Nutritional Information

Calories: 173 Calories from Fat: 36%

Total Fat: 7g Saturated Fat: 1g Cholesterol: 171mg Sodium: 172mg

Carbohydrate: 3g Protein: 23g Fiber: 0g

Exchanges: 3 Lean Meats

ROASTED CARROT SOUP WITH ROMA TOMATOES

A SOUP SO HEALTHY, you'll wonder how it can taste so good.

1½ medium-sized carrots

1 tablespoon of extra virgin
    olive oil

1 lemon, juiced (approximately
    4 tablespoons)

1 white onion

2 roma tomatoes, chopped

2 sprigs of fresh mint, chopped

2 tablespoons of balsamic vinegar

½ tablespoon of butter or
    margarine

3¾ cups of cold water

1 leek (white parts only), sliced

¼ teaspoon of salt (optional)

⅛ teaspoon of freshly ground
    black pepper

1. Preheat oven to 400 degrees. Peel carrots and chop coarsely. Toss with ½ tablespoon of olive oil and 2 tablespoons of lemon juice. Lay flat on a shallow baking sheet and roast for approximately 15 minutes.

2. Meanwhile, halve the onion, dice one half into ¼-inch squares and place on baking sheet with carrots and caramelize carrots and onion for an additional 15-20 minutes. Slice the other half of the onion into half-rings. Set aside.

3. Combine mint, tomatoes, onion rings and balsamic vinegar in a medium mixing bowl. Toss with the remaining ½ tablespoon of olive oil. Set aside.

4. Heat a large saucepan over medium-high heat, add butter or margarine and stir quickly. Add the sliced onion and roasted carrot, stir again. Add the water and leek and boil for 15 minutes. Transfer to a food processor or blend in blender (in batches) and purée until smooth. Return mixture to saucepan and season with salt, pepper and the remaining 2 tablespoons of lemon juice. Heat to desired temperature.

5. To serve, pour soup into bowls. Add the reserved mint and tomato mixture to each bowl.

YIELD: 4 SERVINGS   **PREP TIME:** 30 MIN.   **COOKING TIME:** 1 HOUR

Nutritional
Information

Calories: 103 Calories from Fat: 44%

Total Fat: 5g Saturated Fat: 1g Cholesterol: 2mg Sodium: 180mg

Carbohydrate: 15g Protein: 1g Fiber: 4g

Exchanges: 1 Carb & 1 Fat

GRILLED SALMON PROVENCAL

SALMON IS DELICIOUS and loaded with healthful essential fatty acids.

6 teaspoons of olive oil

¼ teaspoon of salt (optional)

¼ teaspoon of freshly ground black pepper

1 tablespoon of fresh thyme, chopped

2 pounds of red bliss or other small potatoes, halved

For the tomato relish:

½ teaspoon of shallots, chopped

½ teaspoon of garlic, chopped

8 tomatoes (about 1½ pounds), blanched, peeled and de-seeded, cut into quarters

16 Kalamata olives, pitted and halved

1 teaspoon of chives, chopped

4 6-ounce salmon filets, skinned

1. Preheat oven to 350 degrees. Combine 4 teaspoons of the olive oil, salt, pepper and the thyme in a large bowl. Add potatoes and toss until lightly coated. Place potatoes on a baking sheet and roast until golden brown, about 30 minutes.

2. Light the grill. Meanwhile, make the tomato relish: Sauté shallots and garlic in the remaining 2 teaspoons of olive oil until light brown, about 5 minutes. Toss tomatoes, shallot and garlic with the olives. Add the chopped chives. Set aside.

3. Grill the salmon filets until cooked through, but not dry, about 6 minutes on each side. To serve, divide potatoes between four plates, place a salmon filet on top of potatoes. Top with tomato relish. Serve immediately.

YIELD: 4 SERVINGS   **PREP TIME:** 30 MIN.

COOKING TIME: 1 HOUR

▶▶ Nutritional Information

Calories: 424 Calories from Fat: 27%

Total Fat: 13g Saturated Fat: 2g Cholesterol: 66mg Sodium: 222mg

Carbohydrate: 44g Protein: 32g Fiber: 2g

Exchanges: 3 Carbs & 4 Lean Meats

COFFEE AMARETTO PARFAIT

AN EASY WAY to transform plain vanilla ice cream into a festive dish.

¾ cup of coffee, chilled

1½ tablespoons of Amaretto, almond-flavored liqueur, or ½ teaspoon of almond extract

2 cups of vanilla, no sugar added ice cream

1. In a small pitcher, combine the coffee and the amaretto.

2. In each of 4 tall glasses, place ½ cup of the ice cream. Spoon 2 tablespoons of the coffee amaretto mixture over the ice cream. Serve immediately. If desired, a chocolate wafer may be served on top, stuck into the ice cream.

YIELD: 4 SERVINGS   **PREP TIME:** 5 MIN.

▶**TABLE TALK: DESSERTS** It is common to want a dessert to complete your meal. You can fit desserts into your meal plan as long as you account for the carbohydrate and fat calories provided by these treats. To help maintain good blood sugar control:

- Choose a few favorite desserts. Decide how often to eat them and how to fit them into your meal plan

- Eat only a small portion

- Use the nutrition information to learn about the calorie, carbohydrate, fat, saturated fat and cholesterol content of desserts

- When you eat a sweet, check your blood glucose about 2 hours later to see how it has been affected by the treat

Nutritional Information

Calories: 110 Calories from Fat: 41%

Total Fat: 5g Saturated Fat: 2.5g Cholesterol: 5mg Sodium: 514mg

Carbohydrate: 13g Protein: 3g Fiber: 0g

Exchanges: 1 Carb & 1 Fat

AMERICA'S HEARTLAND

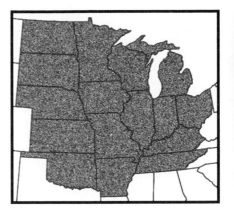

Green pastures and lush golden fields flourish in the lands of the Midwest, providing us with ingredients that have become staples of the American diet. Wisconsin supplies many Americans with rich dairy products, such as milk and cheese, while the Northern lakes provide bountiful freshwater fish. America's Heartland also produces an abundance of corn and wheat, which are found in many traditional Midwestern dishes.

Midwest cooking tends to be simple and straightforward, but often contains a high fat content which may contribute to obesity. Obesity can potentially increase the risk for developing type 2 diabetes. If one or more close relatives have type 2 diabetes, there is nearly a 50 percent chance an individual will develop insulin resistance, an underlying cause of the disease. The good news is that diabetes can be managed with a proper meal plan, regular physical activity and early treatment with medication, when necessary.

In the following chapter, you will find traditional Midwest dishes, such as Seared Flank Steak Salad (page 50) and Lamb Chops with Marinated Vegetables (page 54), that can be prepared more healthily without compromising the taste.

CHEF: HARLAN W. PETERSON

- ▶ **Grilled Vegetable-Stuffed Beef Roulades**
- ▶ **Seared Flank Steak Salad**
- ▶ **New Potato and Green Bean Salad**

CHEF: MARCUS SAMUELSSON

- ▶ **Lamb Chops with Marinated Vegetables**
- ▶ **Roasted Chicken with Spiced Apples and Onions**
- ▶ **Steamed Bass with Carrot Ginger Broth**

CHEF: EMILY LUCHETTI

- ▶ **Raspberry Gratin**

CHEF ▶ HARLAN W. PETERSON

In 1977, Harlan left a career designing automobiles to pursue his passion for food. He began as a hustling apprentice at the Rowe Inn in Ellsworth, Michigan where he was promoted to Executive Chef in 1981. Nominated for Best Chef in the Midwest four times by the James Beard Foundation, Harlan Peterson is a creative master of modern American cooking. Samples of his imaginative cuisine can be found at his unique restaurant Tapawingo, in Ellsworth, Michigan. Tapawingo has been featured often in *Bon Appétit* magazine, and in May 1999 was inaugurated into the Fine Dining Hall of Fame by *Nation's Restaurant News*.

GRILLED VEGETABLE-STUFFED BEEF ROULADES

HERE'S A NIFTY WAY to make beef and vegetables into an exciting dish.

- 4 tablespoons of low-sodium soy sauce
- 2 tablespoons of packed light brown sugar
- 1 pound of beef tenderloin, well-trimmed
- Salt and freshly ground black pepper to taste (optional)
- 4 green onions, green tops cut into 3-inch lengths and sliced lengthwise
- 2 ribs of celery, julienned into ¼-x 4-inch pieces
- 1 each red and yellow bell peppers, trimmed, seeded, and cut into ¼-x 4 inch pieces
- 2 teaspoons of olive oil

1. Light the grill or preheat the broiler. In a small bowl, whisk together the soy sauce and the brown sugar until dissolved. Set aside.

2. Cut the tenderloin crosswise into 8 portions, approximately ½-inch thick slices. Trim off any fat or connective tissue. Place each slice between 2 pieces of plastic wrap. Use the flat side of a meat pounder to pound out each slice, keeping it in a rectangular shape, until it is about ⅛-inch thick. Remove the plastic wrap and transfer the thin slice to a larger plate. Continue until all the beef is pounded. Brush one side (inside) of the beef pieces with the soy sauce mixture and place it on a clean surface. Sprinkle with salt and pepper.

3. Distribute the green onions, celery and pepper slices equally on each piece of beef. Roll up lengthwise, and skewer each roulade with 2 toothpicks so the rolls are taut and will not unroll.

4. Grill or broil the beef rolls, brushing with a little olive oil so they will not stick to the cooking surface. Grill each roll until well browned, and the vegetables inside are hot but not mushy (about 5 minutes, turning once). Serve immediately. May be served with potatoes for dinner or with 4 cups of mixed greens as a luncheon dish.

YIELD: 4 SERVINGS **PREP TIME:** 30 MIN. **COOKING TIME:** 20 MIN.

 Nutritional Information

Calories: 242 Calories from Fat: 37%

Total Fat: 10g Saturated Fat: 3g Cholesterol: 57mg Sodium: 354mg

Carbohydrate: 11g Protein: 25g Fiber: 1g

Exchanges: ½ Carb & 3 Lean Meats

SEARED FLANK STEAK SALAD

A STYLISH AND HEALTHY DISH that will delight your guests.

For the marinade:

2 cloves of garlic, finely chopped

1 sprig of fresh rosemary leaves, chopped

2 sprigs of fresh thyme leaves, chopped

2 fresh sage leaves, chopped

2 fresh basil leaves, chopped

1 teaspoon of freshly ground black pepper

1 tablespoon of olive oil

¼ teaspoon of salt (optional)

16 ounces of flank steak

To make the vinaigrette:

1½ tablespoons of olive oil

1 clove of garlic, minced

2 teaspoons of honey

1 tablespoon of low-sodium soy sauce

1 teaspoon of fresh ginger, peeled and grated

½ teaspoon of rosemary, finely minced

¼ teaspoon of freshly ground black pepper

1½ tablespoons of fresh lemon juice

4 cups of mesclun or mixed baby greens

1. In a small bowl, combine garlic, rosemary, thyme, sage, basil, pepper and olive oil. Trim steak of any fat, if necessary, then rub with herb marinade. Cover and refrigerate overnight or for several hours.

2. Light the grill. Just before cooking, season the meat with a ¼ teaspoon of salt. Cook at high heat for 5 minutes on each side or until medium-rare.

3. Let rest in a warm place for 10 minutes before slicing. Slice thinly on the bias and divide into four equal servings.

4. To make vinaigrette, heat olive oil in a small skillet over medium heat. Add sliced garlic and sauté until cooked through (about 1½ to 2 minutes). Be careful not to burn the garlic. Let oil and garlic cool.

5. In a large bowl, combine cooled oil and garlic with honey, soy sauce, ginger, rosemary and pepper. Whisk to blend. Slowly drizzle in lemon juice, whisking constantly. Set aside.

▶▶ Nutritional Information

Calories: 241 Calories from Fat: 52%

Total Fat: 14 g Saturated Fat: 4g Cholesterol: 34mg Sodium: 193mg

Carbohydrate: 7g Protein: 20g Fiber: 1g

Exchanges: 3 Lean Meats, 1 Vegetable & 1 Fat

6. To serve, toss salad greens with desired amount of vinaigrette. Place greens on each of 4 plates and then fan out slices of steak either on the top or off to the side. Serve immediately.

YIELD: 4 SERVINGS   **PREP TIME:** 6 HOURS 30 MIN. (INCLUDING MARINATING TIME)
COOKING TIME: 25 MIN.

▶ **TABLE TALK: HERBS**   There are many varieties of herbs. Most of them have been used in cooking for centuries. Rosemary, sage, parsley and thyme are a few of the most popular.

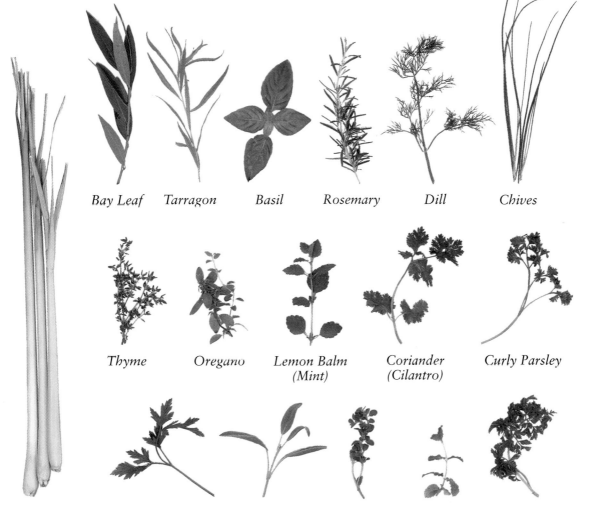

Bay Leaf   Tarragon   Basil   Rosemary   Dill   Chives

Thyme   Oregano   Lemon Balm   Coriander   Curly Parsley
(Mint)   (Cilantro)

Lemon Grass   Italian Parsley   Sage   Marjoram   Mint   Chervil

51

NEW POTATO AND GREEN BEAN SALAD

A WARM SALAD that is loaded with flavor and can double as a main course vegetable.

¾ pound of small new potatoes, quartered or halved

8 ounces of small green beans, stemmed

1½ teaspoons of freshly ground black pepper

2 green onions (scallions), trimmed of the green ends and minced

2 tablespoons of extra virgin olive oil

3 small, ripe tomatoes, cored and cut into sixths

2 tablespoons of fresh basil, chopped

2 tablespoons of red wine vinegar or balsamic vinegar

¼ teaspoon of salt (optional)

1. In a large saucepan of boiling water, cook the potatoes until just tender.

2. Simultaneously, in a separate pan of boiling water, cook the green beans until just crisp-tender, timing so the potatoes and beans are done at the same time.

3. Immediately drain the potatoes and beans and place them both in a large bowl. While the potatoes and beans are still hot, add the pepper, minced green onion and olive oil. Gently toss the vegetables (the vegetables absorb more of the onion and olive oil flavors if they are still hot). Set aside to cool (optional).

4. When ready to serve, add the tomato pieces, basil, vinegar and salt and again gently toss. This salad is best served warm, but is also good served chilled.

YIELD: 4 SERVINGS   PREP TIME: 15 MIN.
COOKING TIME: 30 MIN.

▶▶ Nutritional Information

Calories: 160 Calories from Fat: 39%

Total Fat: 7g Saturated Fat: <1g Cholesterol: 0mg Sodium: 160mg

Carbohydrate: 22g Protein: 3g Fiber: 4g

Exchanges: 1½ Carbs & 1 Fat

CHEF ▶ MARCUS SAMUELSSON

A native Ethiopian, Marcus Samuelsson was adopted by a couple from Göteborg, Sweden. Marcus' grandmother, a professional cook, gave him an early passion for food and taught him the secrets of Swedish cuisine. During apprenticeships in France, Switzerland and Austria, Marcus got a solid training in classic French cuisine. After bringing his culinary mastery to New York at Aquavit restaurant, this young prodigy recently opened a second restaurant in Minneapolis, a dazzling tribute to the city's Scandinavian heritage. In 1999, Marcus was named Rising Star Chef of the Year by the James Beard Foundation.

Lamb Chops with Marinated Vegetables, recipe on page 54

LAMB CHOPS WITH MARINATED VEGETABLES

A COLORFUL AND TASTY DISH from the Heartland.

For the marinated vegetables:

3 garlic cloves, halved

2 shallots, peeled and quartered

20 pear or cherry tomatoes

3 scallions, sliced into 2-inch pieces

½ cup of extra virgin olive oil

¼ cup of lemon juice

3 tablespoons of balsamic vinegar

4 lamb chops (1¼ pounds total)

For the sauce:

1 cup of low-sodium chicken broth

½ cup of fresh basil leaves, chopped

1½ teaspoons of lemon juice

1 teaspoon of butter or margarine

1. In a small bowl, combine garlic, shallots, tomatoes, scallions, olive oil, lemon juice and balsamic vinegar. Marinate for 6 hours or overnight.

2. Preheat the oven to 450 degrees. Remove the vegetables from the marinade and sauté in a medium-sized pan until golden brown, approximately 3 minutes. Set aside and keep warm.

3. Place the lamb on a baking sheet. Bake for 9 minutes, turning once.

4. In a separate saucepan, blend chicken broth, basil leaves and lemon juice. Bring to a boil and add the butter or margarine. To serve, divide the marinated vegetables onto 4 plates. Top with the lamb and drizzle with the sauce.

YIELD: 4 SERVINGS **PREP TIME:** 6 HOURS 15 MIN. (INCLUDING MARINATING TIME)
COOKING TIME: 30 MIN.

▶**TABLE TALK: LAMB CHOPS** Lamb has an excellent nutritional profile, fitting in perfectly with the trend toward lighter, leaner and more healthful foods. A 3-ounce serving of lean lamb contains about 176 calories and just 76 milligrams of cholesterol. Lamb is also high in B vitamins, niacin, zinc and iron.

▶▶ Nutritional Information

Calories: 303 Calories from Fat: 47%

Total Fat: 16g Saturated Fat: 4g Cholesterol: 101mg Sodium: 406mg

Carbohydrate: 7g Protein: 30g Fiber: 1g

Exchanges: 4 Lean Meats, 1 Vegetable & 1 Fat

ROASTED CHICKEN WITH SPICED APPLES AND ONIONS

AMERICANS LOVE CHICKEN because it is so versatile. Here is a wonderful preparation full of flavor and fresh fruitiness.

1 3½ pound free range chicken

1 medium sweet potato, cut into ½-inch cubes

1 onion, cut into ½-inch cubes

2 Granny Smith apples, peeled, cored and cut into ½-inch cubes

2 shallots, cut into ½-inch pieces

1 clove of garlic, chopped

Leaves from 2 sprigs of fresh thyme, chopped

Leaves from 2 sprigs of fresh mint, chopped

1 tablespoon of olive oil

½ teaspoon of ground cinnamon

2 cardamom pods or ⅛ teaspoon of ground cardamom

2 whole cloves or ⅛ teaspoon of ground cloves

4 white peppercorns

2 black peppercorns

¼ teaspoon of kosher salt (optional)

1. Preheat oven to 350 degrees. Rinse chicken with cool water and pat dry with paper towels. Set aside.

2. Fill a medium saucepan half full of water and bring to a boil. Add cubes of sweet potato and blanch for 2 minutes. Drain, rinse with cold water and drain again. In a mixing bowl, combine blanched sweet potato, onion, apples, shallots and garlic. Add chopped thyme and mint leaves. In a small bowl, combine olive oil with 2 tablespoons of water, and add to apple and vegetable mixture.

3. Separately, combine cinnamon, cardamom, cloves, peppercorns and salt. Lightly crush ingredients together with a mortar and pestle, or with the base of a heavy pot on a cutting board, or with a rolling pin over a sealable plastic bag. Add half the spice mixture to the vegetable mixture and reserve the rest.

(continued)

▶ Nutritional Information

Calories: 336 Calories from Fat: 35%

Total Fat: 13g Saturated Fat: 3g Cholesterol: 131mg Sodium: 557mg

Carbohydrate: 21g Protein: 34g Fiber: 3g

Exchanges: 1½ Carbs & 5 Lean Meats

4. Stuff the chicken with some of the vegetables and place the remainder of the vegetables on the bottom of a large roasting pan. Put the chicken into the pan. Sprinkle the remaining spice mixture on the outside of the chicken.

5. Place the pan in the oven and roast the chicken for about 1½ hours or until the internal temperature of the meat reaches 160 degrees. Check pan occasionally, adding a bit of water if it becomes very dry. When vegetables in base of pan are tender, remove and reserve.

6. When the chicken is cooked, remove vegetables from cavity and add to the reserved pan of vegetables. Carve chicken, cover securely and keep warm. Add enough water to the pan juices to make one cup. Place the pan on the stove over medium heat. Bring to a simmer and stir well to deglaze the pan (loosen the bits from the bottom of the pan) and reduce the liquid by half. Use the deglazed pan juices to moisten each serving. Serve.

YIELD: 4 SERVINGS **PREP TIME:** 40 MIN. **COOKING TIME:** 2 HOURS 10 MIN.

▶ **TABLE TALK: A HOLIDAY FEAST** Try this autumn-oriented dish at Thanksgiving instead of the traditional turkey. Interestingly, there is no evidence that turkey was actually served at the first Thanksgiving in 1621, though we do know that alternative items were served including goose, corn bread, oysters – and popcorn, brought by the Indians.

For most people, a healthy diet includes 10 to 20 percent of daily calories from protein (poultry, fish, dairy and vegetable sources) as well as, 50 to 60 percent from carbohydrates (fruits, vegetables, beans and starchy foods such as breads).

To make a complete meal, pair this dish with Southwest Grilled Potatoes (page 36) or Garlic Mashed Potatoes (page 84), and add your favorite vegetable.

STEAMED BASS with carrot ginger broth

A DELICIOUS AND UNUSUAL DISH that makes a perfect focus for a summer luncheon.

For the broth:

½ pound of carrots, coarsely chopped

2 shallots, cut into quarters

2 garlic cloves, halved

4 sprigs of thyme, chopped

1 3-inch piece of ginger, peeled and minced

1 teaspoon of vegetable oil

1 cup of diet ginger ale

1 cup of low-sodium chicken broth

Juice from ½ lemon

4 5-ounce bass filets

2 sprigs of mint

1 3-inch piece of lemongrass, halved lengthwise

Garnish (optional):

2 tablespoons of low-fat sour cream

1. Preheat oven to 350 degrees. To make the carrot ginger broth, put the carrots, shallots, garlic, thyme and ginger on a sheet pan. Drizzle with oil and bake in the oven until soft, about 25 minutes.

2. In a food processor or blender, combine ginger ale, chicken broth and lemon juice. Mix until smooth. Add the softened vegetables and blend until smooth. Transfer mixture into a medium saucepan and simmer for 20 minutes. Set aside to cool.

3. In a steamer, place the bass filets, mint and lemongrass and steam for 4 minutes. Let cool.

4. To serve, pour ½ cup of broth into each of four low-rim soup bowls. Place one filet in each bowl. Serve chilled with ½ tablespoon of sour cream in each bowl.

YIELD: 4 SERVINGS **PREP TIME:** 20 MIN.

COOKING TIME: 1 HOUR 15 MIN.

▶▶ Nutritional Information

Calories: 173 Calories from Fat: 26%

Total Fat: 5g Saturated Fat: 1g Cholesterol: 75mg Sodium: 242mg

Carbohydrate: 3g Protein: 27g Fiber: 2g

Exchanges: 4 Very Lean Meats

RASPBERRY GRATIN

THE PERFECT, low-calorie dessert.

8 ounces of raspberries ½ cup of low-fat sour cream 4 tablespoons of dark brown   sugar

1. Preheat the oven to 400 degrees. Divide raspberries into single layers in four individual, shallow oven proof baking dishes.

2. Gently spread 2 tablespoons of sour cream over each portion of raspberries completely covering them. Sprinkle dark brown sugar over the sour cream, using 1 tablespoon for each dish.

3. Place the dishes on a baking sheet. Bake them in the oven for 5 minutes. Serve immediately.

YIELD: 4 SERVINGS   **PREP TIME:** 20 MIN.   **COOKING TIME:** 5 MIN.

▶**TABLE TALK: RASPBERRIES**

- Each "berry" of the raspberry is actually a cluster of tiny fruits, each with its own seed. Look closely and you can see this.

- Raspberries are very popular with gourmet chefs because of their pungent flavor and striking color.

- Fruits, including raspberries, blueberries and strawberries, are high in fiber and high in vitamins — especially vitamins A and C — and rich in minerals — especially potassium and magnesium.

 Nutritional
Information

Calories: 102 Calories from Fat: 26%

Total Fat: 3g Saturated Fat: 2g Cholesterol: 11.5mg Sodium: 16mg

Carbohydrate: 16.5g Protein: 2g Fiber: 4g

Exchanges: 1 Carb & ½ Fat

A PROUD TRADITION

*B*oston baked beans, Manhattan clam chowder, Vermont maple syrup . . . the spirit of the Northeast is apparent in a number of foods we savor. This spirit dates back to the earliest of times in America. In fact, the most food-oriented holiday, Thanksgiving, is a tribute to the heartiness of Northeastern foods. The original American colonists' foods were adapted to the New World as they learned how to plant corn, gather clams and hunt. Northeasterners look to the Atlantic Ocean for its riches of fish and shellfish. Tomatoes, pumpkins, squash and cranberries also are among the foods associated with the Northeast and New England in particular.

CHEF: **EMILY LUCHETTI**
▶ **Banana Napoleon with Cocoa Sauce**

CHEF: **MICHEL NISCHAN**
▶ **Mushroom, Goat Cheese, and Herb Omelet**
▶ **Pan Roast Chicken with Heirloom Tomatoes**
▶ **New York Clam Chowder**

CHEF: **MARC VETRI**
▶ **Cauliflower and Black Olive Casserole**
▶ **Sautéed Mushrooms on a Bed of Polenta**
▶ **Rigatoni with Broccoli Rabe and Tomatoes**

CHEF: **KENNETH ORINGER**
▶ **Slow Roasted Cod with Clams, Bean Sprouts and Celery Root**
▶ **Asparagus Soup with Maine Lobster**

The following chapter includes appetizing Northeastern recipes that have a lower fat content — an important factor for people who have type 2 diabetes. Developing a meal plan can be as important as physical activity and medication in the treatment of insulin resistance, an underlying cause of type 2 diabetes. When creating a meal plan, you may want to consider combining dishes such as Pan Roast Chicken with Heirloom Tomatoes (page 63) and Sautéed Mushrooms on a Bed of Polenta (page 67) or Rigatoni with Broccoli Rabe (page 68) and Asparagus Soup with Maine Lobster (page 72).

CHEF ▶ EMILY LUCHETTI

BANANA NAPOLEON WITH COCOA SAUCE

A HEALTHY VERSION of an Italian delight, this dessert will bring out the kid in everyone.

For the sauce:

2 tablespoons of cocoa powder

6 tablespoons of water

1½ tablespoons of sugar

For the Napoleon:

6 graham crackers

3 large bananas, sliced into 4-inch pieces on a diagonal

10 tablespoons of light non-dairy whipped topping

1. In a small bowl, whisk together the cocoa powder and 3 tablespoons of water until smooth. Set aside.

2. In a small pot, combine the remaining water with the sugar. Bring the mixture to a boil over medium-high heat. When it comes to a boil, remove from the heat and whisk in the reserved cocoa paste.

3. Return the mixture to the stove and let it cook for one minute, until it thickens slightly. Transfer the sauce to a bowl and refrigerate until cold, about 30 minutes. This sauce can be made in advance.

4. Break the graham crackers in half. You will have 12 two-inch squares. Place one graham cracker square on each of four plates. Place some of the bananas on each graham cracker. Top with 1 tablespoon of whipped topping and then 1 teaspoon of cocoa sauce.

5. Top and repeat with another graham cracker, bananas, whipped topping and cocoa sauce. Place a third graham cracker on top and garnish with ½ tablespoon of whipped topping. Serve immediately.

YIELD: 4 SERVINGS   **PREP TIME:** 20 MIN.   **COOKING TIME:** 45 MIN. (INCLUDING COOLING)

Nutritional Information

Calories: 175 Calories from Fat: 20%

Total Fat: 4g Saturated Fat: 2g Cholesterol: 0mg Sodium: 128mg

Carbohydrate: 34g Protein: 2g Fiber: 1g

Exchanges: 2 Carbs & 1 Fat

Michel Nischan's enthusiasm for food began in his mother's kitchen. According to Michel, her tough standards and respect for nature continue to inspire him today. Michel quickly worked his way through several of Chicago's best French restaurants before he opened his first restaurant, Miche Mache in Connecticut. When his young son Chris was diagnosed with diabetes, Michel became committed to finding healthy foods for people with food-related illnesses. Today, Michel is Executive Chef at the highly successful, health-oriented gourmet restaurant Heartbeat in New York City. His passion for food and life is an example to all who meet him.

MUSHROOM, GOAT CHEESE AND HERB OMELET

A QUICK BRUNCH DISH.

6 shiitake mushrooms, briefly roasted

4 whole eggs

4 egg whites

¼ teaspoon of salt (optional)

¼ teaspoon of freshly ground black pepper

1 teaspoon of grapeseed oil or canola oil

1 teaspoon of parsley, chopped

1 teaspoon of thyme, chopped

1 teaspoon of chives, chopped

2 tablespoons of low-fat goat cheese, crumbled

1. Preheat the broiler. Roast the mushrooms by placing them, rounded side up, in a broiler pan. Broil for 6 minutes, turning until mushrooms are browned and softened. Cut into thin slices and set aside.

2. Combine the eggs and egg whites in a medium mixing bowl and whisk vigorously until well-blended and frothy. Season with salt and pepper.

3. Heat a 10-inch, non-stick skillet over medium-high heat. Once the pan is hot, add the oil and then, immediately, the eggs and mushrooms. Fold in the eggs rapidly, concentrating on moving them from the outside of the pan to the center. Sprinkle in half of the parsley, thyme and chives and continue folding until the omelet begins to set. To serve, remove from heat and sprinkle with goat cheese and the remaining parsley, thyme and chives.

4. You can finish the omelet by placing the pan under a preheated broiler or in a hot (500 degree) oven until the cheese softens.

YIELD: 4 SERVINGS PREP TIME: 15 MIN. COOKING TIME: 35 MIN.

▶▶ Nutritional Information

Calories: 116 Calories from Fat: 46%

Total Fat: 6g Saturated Fat: 3.5g Cholesterol: 214mg Sodium: 326mg

Carbohydrate: 3g Protein: 10g Fiber: 1g

Exchanges: 1½ Medium–Fat Meats

PAN ROAST CHICKEN with HEIRLOOM TOMATOES

AN ALL-AMERICAN CHICKEN DISH that will become a regular in your home.

- 4 skin-on, boneless chicken breasts (about 6 ounces each)
- 4 fresh bay leaves
- ¼ teaspoon of salt (optional)
- ⅛ teaspoon of freshly ground black pepper
- 2 teaspoons of grapeseed oil or canola oil
- 2 cups of low-sodium chicken broth
- 1½ pounds of tomatoes, sliced ½-inch thick
- 2 tablespoons of balsamic vinegar

1. Insert one fresh bay leaf between the skin and meat of each chicken breast. Cover and refrigerate for one hour. Remove and reserve the bay leaves.

2. Heat a large, non-stick sauté pan over medium-low heat until pan is hot. Lightly season each chicken breast with salt and pepper on both sides. Rub the oil onto the skin of each chicken breast and place the breasts, skin-side down into the hot sauté pan. Turn the heat up to medium and allow the breasts to cook until well-browned. Turn the chicken breasts over.

3. Add the chicken broth and simmer for 3 to 5 minutes or until chicken is cooked through. Remove chicken breasts from the pan, reserving the broth. Remove skin from chicken and keep warm.

4. Add the tomatoes to the chicken broth and simmer until they heat through. Swirl the pan, rather than stirring, so the tomatoes retain their individual shape and color. Remove from the heat immediately and swirl in the reserved bay leaves. Add balsamic vinegar.

5. To serve, spoon the tomatoes with sauce into the centers of four plates. Place chicken breasts over the sauce, garnish with the bay leaves.

YIELD: 4 SERVINGS PREP TIME: 1 HOUR 25 MIN. COOKING TIME: 35 MIN.

 Nutritional Information

Calories: 203 Calories from Fat: 26%

Total Fat: 6g Saturated Fat: 1g Cholesterol: 79mg Sodium: 480mg

Carbohydrate: 9g Protein: 26g Fiber: 2g

Exchanges: ½ Carb & 3 Lean Meats

63

NEW YORK CLAM CHOWDER

THE NEW YORK VERSION is characterized by its intense red color and hearty tomato flavor.

1 tablespoon of grapeseed or canola oil

1 medium onion, diced

2 small cloves of garlic, chopped

2 celery stalks, diced

½ cup of dry white wine

4 small, ripe red tomatoes, peeled and chopped

3 cups of chopped clams with juice or 5 6½-ounce cans

1 cup of bottled clam juice

1 cup of water

4 ounces of blanched potatoes, peeled and diced

2 tablespoons of fresh thyme leaves

¼ teaspoon of salt (optional)

⅛ teaspoon of freshly ground black pepper

1. Heat the oil in a heavy-bottomed pot. Add the onion, garlic and celery and sauté until the garlic and onion begin to soften but not brown.

2. Add the white wine and bring to a boil. Cook until the wine reduces by half. Add the tomatoes, clams, clam juice, water, and potatoes. Simmer for 15–20 minutes.

3. Remove from the heat, add the freshly picked thyme leaves, and season with salt and pepper. Serve.

YIELD: 4–6 SERVINGS

PREP TIME: 20 MIN.

COOKING TIME: 40 MIN.

▶ **TABLE TALK: CHOWDERS** Chowder usually means a thick soup containing fish or clams and cream. Cream is not a necessary ingredient and can easily be eliminated to make the soup low-fat. In fact, there are several versions of chowder found in Rhode Island and Manhattan that incorporate tomatoes instead of cream to make a vibrant, hearty version of the traditional New England clam chowder soup.

▶▶ Nutritional Information

Calories: 160 Calories from Fat: 23%

Total Fat: 4g Saturated Fat: <1g Cholesterol: 38.5mg Sodium: 264mg

Carbohydrate: 12g Protein: 15g Fiber: 1.5g

Exchanges: 1 Carb & 2 Lean Meats

Voted one of *Food & Wine* magazine's Ten Best New American Chefs in 1999, Marc Vetri has perfected a rustic Italian technique that is completely distinctive and entirely his own. Co-owner and Executive Chef of the highly acclaimed Vetri in Philadelphia, this master has spent several years in Italy and New York honing his craft. Born into a family of accomplished restaurateurs, Marc has worked with many of the greats, including the world-famous Wolfgang Puck. Today, Vetri restaurant is so popular that Philadelphians must book reservations months in advance for the chance to enjoy Marc's singular Italian cooking.

CAULIFLOWER AND BLACK OLIVE CASSEROLE

A LOVELY VEGETARIAN COMBINATION that is a great lunch dish.

1 pound of cauliflower (approximately 1 head or 11 florets)

1 small onion, minced

1 tablespoon of olive oil

10 black olives, pitted and quartered (preferably Gaeta)

¼ teaspoon of salt (optional)

⅛ teaspoon of freshly ground black pepper

¼ cup of grated pecorino cheese or non-fat parmesan

1. Preheat oven to 375 degrees. Cut cauliflower into 2-inch florets and boil in water for 3 to 4 minutes. Drain and set aside.

2. Separately, sauté the onion over medium heat in ½ tablespoon of the olive oil until golden, about 6–8 minutes. Remove from heat and add olives.

3. Arrange the boiled cauliflower evenly in a casserole. Add the olive and onion mixture, salt and pepper. Drizzle with the remaining olive oil and sprinkle with the cheese. Place the casserole in the oven and bake for 20 minutes.

YIELD: 4 SERVINGS **PREP TIME:** 20 MIN. **COOKING TIME:** 45 MIN.

Nutritional Information

Calories: 118 Calories from Fat: 53%

Total Fat: 7g Saturated Fat: 1.5g Cholesterol: 5mg Sodium: 388mg

Carbohydrate: 10g Protein: 5g Fiber: 2g

Exchanges: 2 Vegetables & 1½ Fats

SAUTÉED MUSHROOMS ON A BED OF POLENTA

A LUSCIOUS VEGETARIAN SIDE DISH.

3 cups of water
¼ teaspoon of salt (optional)
1 cup of ground yellow cornmeal or polenta
3 sprigs of rosemary, chopped
2 cups of mushrooms (or mushroom tops), sliced
1 tablespoon of olive oil
1 clove of garlic, minced
1 small onion, minced
1 tablespoon of red wine vinegar

1. In a large pot, boil 2½ cups of the water and salt. Slowly whisk in the cornmeal or polenta. Reduce heat to low while stirring with a wooden spoon. Cook for 40 minutes (or use instant and cook for 5 minutes).

2. Add half of the rosemary to the polenta and cook for an additional five minutes.

3. In a medium saucepan, sauté mushrooms with olive oil for 1 minute over medium heat. Add minced garlic and onion. Keep stirring over medium heat until the onions are soft. If the vegetables become dry, add ½ cup of water. Add vinegar and remaining half of the rosemary.

4. To serve, divide the polenta, which should be moist and creamy, onto four plates and spoon mushroom mixture over the top.

YIELD: 4 SERVINGS **PREP TIME:** 15 MIN. **COOKING TIME:** 1 HOUR 10 MIN.

▶ **TABLE TALK: POLENTA** Polenta is a corn-based porridge that is very popular in Italian cooking. Before corn was introduced to Europe, polenta was made from chestnut flour or barley. When dried polenta becomes solid, it can be cut into squares and other shapes.

▶▶ Nutritional Information

Calories: 168 Calories from Fat: 26%

Total Fat: 5g Saturated Fat: <1g Cholesterol: 0mg Sodium: 149mg

Carbohydrate: 29g Protein: 4g Fiber: 2g

Exchanges: 2 Carbs & 1 Fat

RIGATONI WITH BROCCOLI RABE AND TOMATOES

PASTA AND VEGETABLES are a delightful and flavorful combination.

1 pound of fresh broccoli rabe

1 clove of garlic, minced

2 tablespoons of olive oil

1 cup of tomatoes, diced

¼ teaspoon of salt (optional)

⅛ teaspoon of freshly ground
   black pepper

½ pound of rigatoni

¼ cup of grated low-fat
   parmesan cheese

1. Coarsely chop the broccoli rabe. Cook in boiling water for 3 minutes, until tender-crisp and drain.

2. Return broccoli rabe to pot and sauté with garlic and olive oil for one minute. Add the tomatoes, salt and pepper and cook for another minute.

3. Separately, cook the pasta in water until al dente (cooked just enough to retain a some-what firm texture). Drain the pasta and toss with a tablespoon of the pasta water.

4. To serve, sprinkle the cheese in a bowl and add the vegetables, then the pasta. Toss like a salad. Serve warm.

YIELD: 4 SERVINGS **PREP TIME:** 15 MIN. **COOKING TIME:** 25 MIN.

▶ **TABLE TALK: PASTA** The key to healthy living is moderation. You too can enjoy America's favorite food, pasta, by sticking to two basic rules:

- Control the portion size of your pasta dish so that you can monitor its effect on your blood sugar level.

- The way pasta is cooked makes a difference in the carbohydrate content. In fact, the longer pasta cooks, the more water it absorbs, and the fewer carbohydrate calories remain. For example, one cup of al dente pasta contains 44 grams of carbo-hydrate, whereas 1 cup of pasta cooked tender contains 32 grams of carbohydrate.

▶▶ Nutritional Information

Calories: 333 Calories from Fat: 27%

Total Fat: 10g Saturated Fat: 2g Cholesterol: 5mg Sodium: 298mg

Carbohydrate: 49.5g Protein: 13g Fiber: 6g

Exchanges: 3 Carbs & 2 Fats

CHEF ▶ KENNETH ORINGER

At age 10, Kenneth Oringer began creating sauces from scratch. Today, this versatile virtuoso is considered one of the best contemporary chefs in America. After graduating as "Most Likely to Succeed" from the Culinary Institute of America, Ken began a professional career that has led him to many top restaurants, including the well-known River Café in New York and Silks Restaurant in San Francisco. Along the way, he perfected his skills and learned to blend Asian accents into his cuisine. Ken, who is co-owner and chef at Clio in Boston, was named Best Newcomer of the Year by *Gourmet* in 1997.

SLOW ROASTED COD WITH CLAMS, BEAN SPROUTS AND CELERY ROOT

A TRUE NEW ENGLAND SPECIALTY.

1½ cups of low-sodium vegetable or chicken broth

1½ cups water

4 4-ounce portions of cod (boneless and skinless)

½ pound of clams, steamed, opened and reserved (12 littleneck clams)

1 cup of assorted chopped herbs - tarragon, parsley, chives, thyme

1 large piece of ginger, peeled and cut into a thin julienne

1 lemon, zested

¼ teaspoon of salt (optional)

⅛ teaspoon of freshly ground black pepper   *(continued)*

1. In a 12-inch sauté pan over medium heat, combine 1 cup of the broth and 1 cup of water. Place fish in pan and surround with clams. Add herbs, ginger and lemon zest to fish and season with salt and pepper. Cover with a lid and bring to a simmer. Cook approximately 6 minutes until fish is just cooked.

2. Remove the fish and clams from the broth. Continue to cook the broth mixture until reduced by half. Set both aside and keep warm.

3. In a medium-sized sauté pot, place celery root, remaining ½ cup of chicken broth, ½ cup of water and honey. Cover and place over medium-high heat until celery root is very soft and all the liquid has been absorbed. Roughly mash with a potato masher and set aside.

Nutritional Information

Calories: 269 Calories from Fat: 27%

Total Fat: 8g Saturated Fat: <1g Cholesterol: 56mg Sodium: 396mg

Carbohydrate: 20g Protein: 26g Fiber: 3g

Exchanges: 1 Carb, 3 Lean Meats & 1 Vegetable

CELEBRITY CHEFS ACROSS AMERICA

1 celery root, peeled and cut into
   1-inch pieces

1 tablespoon of honey

2 tablespoons of canola oil

1 pound of bean sprouts

For the vinaigrette:

2 tablespoons of rice wine vinegar

¼ cup of fresh marjoram, chopped

1 cup of tomato, seeded and chopped

4. Heat a small sauté pan until smoking. Add ½ tablespoon of canola oil and bean sprouts. Stir-fry until bean sprouts are just wilted. Set aside.

5. To make the vinaigrette, combine rice wine vinegar, 1½ tablespoons of canola oil, marjoram and 1 tablespoon of warm water in a medium-sized bowl. Mix with a whisk. Stir in tomatoes.

6. To serve, place ½ cup of mashed celery root in the center of each of four dinner plates. Put bean sprouts on top of celery root and place cod on top of that. Place clams around fish. Drizzle with herb vinaigrette, more herbs and the stock reduction from the initial cooking of the fish.

YIELD: 4 SERVINGS   **PREP TIME:** 30 MIN.   **COOKING TIME:** 45 MIN.

ASPARAGUS SOUP WITH MAINE LOBSTER

THE HERBAL FLAVOR of asparagus is a good match for the sweetness of the lobster meat.

1 leek, washed and chopped (including green tops)

3 shallots, peeled and chopped

2 tablespoons of canola oil

¾ cup of water

¼ teaspoon of salt (optional)

¼ teaspoon of freshly ground black pepper

1 cup of low-sodium vegetable or chicken broth

1 pound of asparagus, cut into 1-inch pieces, ends discarded (reserve 12 tips for garnish)

8 ounces of lobster meat, cooked and shelled (frozen is fine)

Garnish (optional):

1 sprig of lemon thyme, chopped

1 sprig of parsley, chopped

1. In a large saucepan, combine leek, shallots, canola oil, ¼ cup of the water, salt and pepper. Cover with foil and simmer over low heat until all vegetables are soft, approximately 30 minutes.

2. In a separate pot, bring broth to a boil and set aside.

3. Add the asparagus to the leek mixture and cook until al dente (cooked just enough to retain a somewhat firm texture). Add this mixture to a blender with reserved broth and remaining ½ cup of water, and purée until smooth.

4. Strain through a fine sieve and force out as much liquid as possible. To serve, mound lobster in four low-rim soup bowls. Ladle soup around and garnish each with lemon thyme, parsley and asparagus tips.

YIELD: 4 SERVINGS **PREP TIME:** 20 MIN. **COOKING TIME:** 50 MIN.

Nutritional Information

Calories: 200 **Calories from Fat:** 36%

Total Fat: 8g **Saturated Fat:** <1g **Cholesterol:** 53mg **Sodium:** 428mg

Carbohydrate: 17g **Protein:** 15g **Fiber:** 1.5g

Exchanges: 1 Carb & 2 Lean Meats

REGION OF DIVERSITY

ith its blend of English, African and Native American traditions, the Southeast is home to some of the most diverse cuisines in America. French-speaking settlers in Louisiana introduced a European flair, including a variety of rich sauces. A Latin flavor has been added to dishes that include fresh seafood, tropical fruits and Caribbean spices. The Southeast also is famous for soul food, including fried chicken and corn bread.

The Southeast has a long tradition of fried foods and rich sauces, so it may not be surprising that the region has a high incidence of type 2 diabetes. In fact, approximately five percent of Southeasterners have been diagnosed with the disease. Insulin resistance, an underlying cause of the disease, often appears before the rise in blood sugar that marks the onset of diabetes. Drugs that directly treat insulin resistance, such as Avandia® (rosiglitazone maleate), have been developed that can help the body use its own insulin more effectively.

Use the following chapter to help you prepare meal plans. You may want to try recipes such as Shrimp and Eggplant Caponata (page 75) or Smothered Pork Chops with Collard Greens (page 83), which combine a variety of spices and flavors.

CHEF: **FRANK BRIGTSEN**
▶ **Shrimp and Eggplant Caponata**
▶ **Cajun Boiled Brisket**
▶ **Creole Baked Fish**

CHEF: **FRANCISCO "PACO" DUARTE**
▶ **Arroz Con Pollo**
▶ **Zarzuela Catalana**
▶ **Gazpacho Andaluz**

CHEF: **EMILY LUCHETTI**
▶ **Baked Peaches with Vanilla Ice Cream**

CHEF: **MICHEL NISCHAN**
▶ **Smothered Pork Chops with Collard Greens**
▶ **Garlic Mashed Potatoes**
▶ **Scrambled Eggs with Cheese Grits**

CHEF ▶ FRANK BRIGTSEN

Frank Brigtsen is at the forefront of a new generation of Louisiana chefs who are revitalizing Creole and Cajun cooking. Schooled under the internationally acclaimed chef Paul Prudhomme, Frank learned his craft at two of New Orleans's most respected restaurants, the Commander's Palace and K-Paul's Louisiana Kitchen, where he quickly moved up the ranks to Executive Chef. Frank Brigtsen currently applies an inventive personal touch by bringing a modern vision to classic Louisiana cooking as the Co-Owner and Executive Chef of the world-famous Brigtsen's in New Orleans.

SHRIMP AND EGGPLANT CAPONATA

A DELIGHTFUL APPETIZER that will provide a flavorful opening to any meal.

1 tablespoon of olive oil

1 cup of celery, diced (½-inch pieces)

1½ cups of yellow onion, diced (½-inch pieces)

2 bay leaves

¾ cup of peeled medium-sized shrimp (about 4½ ounces)

1 12-ounce can of plum tomatoes, diced

2 teaspoons of garlic, minced

½ teaspoon of salt (optional)

¼ teaspoon of freshly ground black pepper

½ teaspoon of dried whole-leaf oregano

3 cups of eggplant, peeled and diced (½-inch pieces)

2 teaspoons of fresh basil, finely chopped

2 tablespoons of red wine vinegar

1 tablespoon of capers, rinsed and drained

2 tablespoons of pine nuts

1. Heat the olive oil in a heavy-duty skillet over medium heat. Add the celery, onions, and bay leaves. Cook, stirring constantly, until the onions become soft and clear, about 8-10 minutes.

2. Add the shrimp, tomatoes, garlic, salt, pepper and oregano. Cook, stirring constantly for 1-2 minutes. Add the eggplant and reduce heat to low. Cover and cook, stirring occasionally, until the eggplant becomes soft and tender, about 8-10 minutes.

(continued)

Nutritional Information

Calories: 167 Calories from Fat: 38%

Total Fat: 7g Saturated Fat: 1g Cholesterol: 48mg Sodium: 685mg

Carbohydrate: 14g Protein: 14g Fiber: 4g

Exchanges: 1 Carb & 2 Lean Meats

3. Add the basil, vinegar, capers, and pine nuts (to toast pine nuts, swirl in a hot pan for 2–3 minutes). Blend thoroughly and remove from heat. Remove the bay leaves before serving. This dish may be served hot, cold or at room temperature.

YIELD: 4 SERVINGS   **PREP TIME:** 45 MIN.   **COOKING TIME:** 40 MIN.

CAJUN BOILED BRISKET

A HEARTY MAIN DISH with a delightful touch of peppery spice. This makes a wonderful family dinner and the leftovers are great in sandwiches.

2 pound beef brisket, trimmed of
    excess fat

1 gallon of cold water

3 cups of yellow onion, diced

2 cups of celery, diced

1 cup of carrots, diced

1 16-ounce can of tomato purée

3 bay leaves

½ teaspoon of kosher salt (optional)

2 tablespoons of garlic, minced

1½ teaspoons of crushed red pepper flakes

1 tablespoon of whole black peppercorns

2 tablespoons of whole coriander seeds

2 tablespoons of whole mustard seeds

1. Place beef brisket and cold water in a large pot. Add water, onion, celery, carrots, tomato purée, bay leaves, salt, garlic, red pepper flakes, black peppercorns, coriander seeds and mustard seeds and bring to a boil. Cover the pot, reduce the heat to low, and simmer until the beef is fork-tender, about 3½ to 4 hours.

2. Turn off the heat and let the brisket rest, covered for 1 hour. This will allow the meat to absorb the seasonings. To serve, slice thinly against the grain. Spoon a little bit of the cooking liquid over the meat.

YIELD: 4 SERVINGS   **PREP TIME:** 20 MIN.   **COOKING TIME:** 5 HOURS 15 MIN.

▶▶ Nutritional Information

Calories: 499 Calories from Fat: 50%

Total Fat: 28g Saturated Fat: 8g Cholesterol: 92mg Sodium: 560mg

Carbohydrate: 34g Protein: 31g Fiber: 8g

Exchanges: 2 Carbs, 4 Medium-Fat Meats & 1½ Fats

CREOLE BAKED FISH

THIS SUPERB PREPARATION will make a special main dish.

1 teaspoon of olive oil
¾ cup of celery, finely diced
¼ cup of green bell pepper, finely diced
¼ cup of yellow bell pepper, finely diced
1 cup of yellow onion, finely diced
1 bay leaf
½ teaspoon of kosher salt (optional)
½ teaspoon of crushed red pepper flakes
1 teaspoon of fresh thyme, finely chopped
2 teaspoons of garlic, minced
½ teaspoon of lemon zest, finely chopped
½ teaspoon of orange zest, finely chopped
1 teaspoon of fresh lemon juice
4 teaspoons of fresh orange juice
1 16-20-ounce can of no-salt-added plum
    tomatoes, finely diced with their juices
1 teaspoon of granulated white sugar
½ cup of water
1 tablespoon of fresh basil, finely chopped
1 tablespoon of fresh oregano, finely chopped
4 5-ounce fresh mild fish filets (redfish,
    snapper, catfish, halibut, or bass)

1. Preheat the oven to 350 degrees. Heat the oil in a saucepan over high heat. Add the celery, green and yellow bell peppers, onions and bay leaf. Cook, stirring constantly, until the onions become soft and transparent (clear), about 8-10 minutes. Reduce heat to low.

2. Add salt, crushed red pepper, thyme, garlic, lemon zest, and orange zest. Cook for 1 minute, stirring constantly. Add lemon juice, orange juice, tomatoes, sugar, and water. Bring mixture to a boil and reduce heat to low.

3. Add the basil and oregano and simmer, stirring occasionally, for 20 minutes. Remove from heat and set aside.

4. Place fish filets in a shallow baking pan and top with the sauce. Place pan in oven and bake until the fish is cooked through, about 15-20 minutes. Serve immediately.

YIELD: 4 SERVINGS **PREP TIME:** 55 MIN. **COOKING TIME:** 1 HOUR

 Nutritional Information

Calories: 209 Calories from Fat: 12%

Total Fat: 3g Saturated Fat: <1g Cholesterol: 52.5mg Sodium: 403mg

Carbohydrate: 13g Protein: 31g Fiber: 2.5g

Exchanges: 1 Carb & 4 Very Lean Meats

CHEF ▶ Francisco "Paco" Duarte

One of the world's most accomplished Spanish chefs, Francisco "Paco" Duarte has been dazzling food lovers worldwide for over 30 years. Born in Cádiz, Spain, Paco is presently the Executive Chef of the oldest Spanish restaurant in the United States, the spectacular Columbia Restaurant in Ybor City, Florida. Following years of intense study abroad, Paco has been instrumental in the award-winning restaurant's success. He is quite proud of the fact that Columbia Restaurant was honored with a "Five Forks" rating by the government of Spain as the "Outstanding Spanish Restaurant in America."

ARROZ CON POLLO

THIS TRADITIONAL SPANISH DISH is inexpensive, low in fat and absolutely delicious.

2 tablespoons of olive oil

3½ pound chicken, cut in quarters

2 medium onions, chopped

1 green pepper, chopped

4 cloves of garlic, minced

2 bay leaves

1 cup of white wine

2 medium tomatoes, peeled, seeded and chopped

½ teaspoon of saffron

¼ teaspoon of salt (optional)

½ teaspoon of freshly ground black pepper

½ teaspoon of ground cumin

1 cube of low-sodium chicken bouillon

2 cups of hot water

¾ cup of long grain rice, uncooked

Garnish (optional):

½ cup of cooked green peas

2 red pimento peppers, cut into strips

1. Preheat oven to 350 degrees. In a casserole, heat the olive oil and sauté the chicken until the skin is golden brown. Remove chicken and set aside.

2. Add the onions, green pepper, garlic, and bay leaves to the casserole and sauté until the onions are transparent (clear), about 5 minutes. Add white wine, tomatoes, saffron, salt, ground pepper and cumin and bring to a boil for 3 minutes.

3. Separately, whisk the bouillon cube in the hot water until dissolved. Add the chicken bouillon and chicken to the casserole and boil for 5 minutes.

4. Add the rice, stir and cover the casserole. Bake in the oven for 20 minutes. When done the rice should be plump and the liquid should all be absorbed. To serve, remove the skin from the chicken and the bay leaf from the rice. Garnish with peas and pimentos.

YIELD: 4 SERVINGS **PREP TIME:** 40 MIN.

COOKING TIME: 1 HOUR

SOUTHEAST

► Nutritional Information

Calories: 503 Calories from Fat: 30%

Total Fat: 17g Saturated Fat: 3g Cholesterol: 119mg Sodium: 343mg

Carbohydrate: 43g Protein: 42g Fiber: 1g

Exchanges: 3 Carbs, 4 Lean Meats & 1 Fat

ZARZUELA CATALANA

THIS IS A DRAMATIC AND FESTIVE Spanish seafood dish with rich and spicy flavors.

4 tablespoons of olive oil

4 cloves of fresh garlic, chopped

1 medium onion, finely chopped

3 medium ripe tomatoes, peeled, seeded and diced

¼ teaspoon of salt (optional)

¼ teaspoon of freshly ground black pepper

2 bay leaves

8 large shrimp, peeled and de-veined

8 scallops

1 lobster tail (about 4 ounces)

8 clams

8 mussels

1 ounce of brandy

2 teaspoons of Spanish paprika

3 ounces of white wine

1. Heat olive oil in skillet. Add the garlic and onion and sauté over low heat. When the onion is transparent (clear), about 8 minutes, add tomatoes, salt, pepper and bay leaves, and bring to a boil. Cook for 2 minutes.

2. Add the shrimp, scallops, lobster tail, clams, mussels and brandy. Flambé (tilt the pan away from you and carefully light the surface of the liquid with a match) to burn off the alcohol. Add paprika and white wine, cover and cook for 5 minutes.

3. Remove lobster tail from shell and slice lengthwise into 4 pieces. To serve, remove bay leaves and divide lobster and seafood mixture among four plates.

YIELD: 4 SERVINGS   **PREP TIME:** 25 MIN.
COOKING TIME: 25 MIN.

▶**TABLE TALK: SEAFOOD** Many types of fish and shellfish contain polyunsaturated fats. These fats are healthier than saturated fats, and an essential part of any meal plan. Thirty percent or less of your daily calories should come from fat, 10 percent of which should come from polyunsaturated fats (fats from fish and other seafood).

▶▶ Nutritional Information

Calories: 293 Calories from Fat: 49%

Total Fat: 16g Saturated Fat: 2g Cholesterol: 67mg Sodium: 314mg

Carbohydrate: 11g Protein: 19g Fiber: 1.5g

Exchanges: 1 Carb, 3 Lean Meats & 1½ Fats

GAZPACHO ANDALUZ

A CRISP, TRADITIONAL cold Spanish soup.

For the soup:

1 cucumber, peeled and chopped

3 ripe tomatoes, peeled and chopped

1 small onion, chopped

1 green pepper, chopped

3 fresh cloves of garlic

2 slices of white bread, cut in pieces

1 teaspoon of ground cumin

2 teaspoons of Spanish paprika

¼ cup of red wine vinegar

2 tablespoons of olive oil

1 18 ounce can of low-sodium
    tomato juice (2¼ cups)

2 cups of cold water

¼ teaspoon of salt (optional)

Garnish (optional):

1 small tomato peeled, seeded and
    diced

1 small onion, diced

1 small green pepper, seeded and diced

1 cup of small croutons (optional)

1 small cucumber peeled, seeded
    and diced

1. Combine cucumber, tomatoes, onion, green pepper, garlic, bread, cumin, paprika, vinegar, olive oil, tomato juice, water and salt in a large bowl.

2. Purée in a blender in 2 batches. Return to the bowl and chill in the refrigerator for at least an hour.

3. For the garnish, combine tomatoes, onion, green peppers, croutons and cucumber in a small bowl.

4. To serve, pour chilled soup in bowls and top with the garnish.

PREP TIME: 25 MIN.

▶▶ Nutritional
Information

Calories: 234 Calories from Fat: 32%

Fat: 8.5g Saturated Fat: 1g Cholesterol: 0mg Sodium: 290mg

Carbohydrate: 36g Protein: 6g Fiber: 5g

Exchanges: 2½ Carbs & 1½ Fats

BAKED PEACHES WITH VANILLA ICE CREAM

A DELICIOUS AND EASY dessert that will delight your whole family.

> 2 large fresh white or yellow
>   peaches (about 15 ounces)
> 2 teaspoons of brown sugar
> 1 teaspoon of unsalted butter
> 2 cups of vanilla, no sugar added
>   ice cream
> 3 vanilla wafer cookies, crushed

1. Preheat the oven to 350 degrees. Cut the peaches in half and remove the pits. Place the peaches, cut side up, in an oven proof dish.

2. Sprinkle ½ teaspoon of brown sugar over each peach half. Dot each peach with ¼ teaspoon of butter.

3. Cut a piece of parchment paper the size of the baking pan. Spray it with non-stick spray. Place the parchment paper, greased side down on top of the peaches. Bake the peaches for 15 minutes.

4. Remove the peaches from the oven. To serve, divide the peach halves between four plates. Top with ½ cup of vanilla ice cream. Sprinkle the crushed vanilla wafers on top. Serve immediately.

YIELD: 4 SERVINGS **PREP TIME:** 25 MIN. **COOKING TIME:** 15 MIN.

▶**TABLE TALK: PEACHES** California produces about half of the peaches harvested in America, with the Southern states of South Carolina and Georgia following. These states provide the best climates for peaches to grow because peaches need to ripen on the tree in order to be at their best and they require a certain number of "chill" days in order to thrive.

▶▶ Nutritional Information

Calories: 165 Calories from Fat: 33%

Total Fat: 6g Saturated Fat: 3g Cholesterol: 8mg Sodium: 67mg

Carbohydrate: 26g Protein: 3g Fiber: 2g

Exchanges: 1½ Carbs & 1 Fat

CHEF ▶ **MICHEL NISCHAN**

SMOTHERED PORK CHOPS WITH COLLARD GREENS

THIS TAKES A LITTLE TIME, but the result is so tasty you'll see why it's worth it.

4 center cut pork shoulder chops, trimmed (approximately 1 pound), cut in half

¼ teaspoon of salt (optional)

⅛ teaspoon of freshly ground black pepper

2 tablespoons of all-purpose flour

2 tablespoons of grapeseed or canola oil

2 medium onions, sliced into ¼-inch pieces

3 green peppers, seeded and sliced into ¼-inch pieces

3 cups of low-sodium chicken broth

For collard greens:

2 cups of low-sodium chicken broth

1 large bunch of collard greens (1 pound), stems removed, chopped into 4-inch pieces

1 large onion, peeled and sliced

1 jalapeño pepper, split in half lengthwise

¼ teaspoon of salt (optional)

⅛ teaspoon of freshly ground black pepper

1 tablespoon of malt vinegar

1. Preheat the oven to 300 degrees. Season each chop with salt and pepper. Pour 1 tablespoon of flour onto a plate. Dip each chop into the flour and shake off the excess.

2. In a heavy skillet over medium heat, heat oil. Place pork chops in the skillet and cook until the chops are well browned — approximately 4 minutes per side. Remove the chops from the skillet and set aside.

3. Add the onions and peppers to the skillet and increase the heat to medium-high. Sprinkle remaining tablespoon of flour on vegetables and cook, stirring constantly for 5 minutes until vegetables are brown.

4. Remove skillet from heat and gradually stir in 3 cups of low-sodium chicken broth until slightly thickened and smooth. Bury the pork chops in the gravy. Cover the skillet and place in the oven. Cook for 2 hours or until pork is tender.

(continued)

Nutritional Information

Calories: 490 Calories from Fat: 43%

Total Fat: 23.5g Saturated Fat: 6g Cholesterol: 102mg Sodium: 630mg

Carbohydrate: 38g Protein: 39g Fiber: 3g

Exchanges: 2½ Carbs & 4 Medium-Fat Meats

5. To prepare collard greens, add 2 cups of chicken broth to a large pot over medium-high heat, bring to a rapid simmer. Add collard greens to the broth with the onion and jalapeño. Reduce heat and simmer for 2 hours. Season with salt, pepper and malt vinegar.

6. To serve, divide the greens onto four plates. Top with pork chops and spoon leftover gravy from the chops over each serving.

YIELD: 4 SERVINGS **PREP TIME:** 30 MIN. **COOKING TIME:** 2 HOURS 30 MIN.

GARLIC MASHED POTATOES

THIS IS SO GOOD you may want to double the recipe so you're sure to have leftovers.

4 whole potatoes (approximately 20 ounces), peeled and cut into 2-inch pieces

4 medium garlic cloves

¼ cup of warm low-fat milk (1%)

2 tablespoons of extra virgin olive oil

½ teaspoon of salt (optional)

¼ teaspoon of freshly ground black pepper

1. Place the potatoes in a medium pot. Add just enough water to cover the potatoes. Bring to a simmer over medium heat. Cook until the potatoes are just tender enough to give only slight resistance when pierced with a knife. Drain well and return to the pot. Place the pot over low heat and cook a minute or two to dry the potatoes out. Set aside.

2. Roast the garlic cloves in a skillet over medium heat, shaking occasionally. Remove from heat and mash into a paste.

3. Add garlic paste, milk and olive oil to the reserved potatoes and mix well. Run through a food mill, or mash with a masher or the back of a spoon to the desired consistency. Season with salt and pepper. Serve.

YIELD: 6 SERVINGS **PREP TIME:** 20 MIN. **COOKING TIME:** 30 MIN.

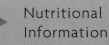

Nutritional Information

Calories: 127 Calories from Fat: 28%

Total Fat: 4g Saturated Fat: <1g Cholesterol: <1mg Sodium: 181 mg

Carbohydrate: 15.5g Protein: 3g Fiber: 2g

Exchanges: 1 Carb & 1 Fat

SCRAMBLED EGGS with CHEESE GRITS

A DOWN HOME PREPARATION that is great for breakfast.

For the grits:

1½ cups of water

¼ teaspoon of salt (optional)

½ cup of stone-ground grits

½ cup of grated, low-fat
  cheddar cheese

1 whole egg

3 whole eggs

2 egg whites

1 tablespoon of grapeseed
  or canola oil

1. Preheat oven to 375 degrees. To prepare grits, bring the water to a simmer in a small pot over medium-high heat. Add the salt, then slowly stir the grits into the simmering water. Cook covered, stirring often until the grits are done (about 45 minutes). Stir in the cheddar cheese, then 1 whole egg and mix well.

2. Spray a small casserole dish with non-stick spray coating and transfer the grits to the casserole. Bake grits until golden brown on top, about 15 minutes.

3. To prepare eggs, combine 3 whole eggs and 2 egg whites in a medium mixing bowl and whisk vigorously until well-blended.

4. Heat the oil in a 10-inch non-stick skillet over high heat. Add the eggs to the skillet and scramble until cooked to your liking. Serve with baked cheese grits.

YIELD: 4 SERVINGS   **PREP TIME:** 15 MIN.
COOKING TIME: 1 HOUR 10 MIN.

▶▶ Nutritional Information

Calories: 215 Calories from Fat: 46%

Total Fat: 11g Saturated Fat: 3g Cholesterol: 222mg Sodium: 333mg

Carbohydrate: 15g Protein: 13g Fiber: <1g

Exchanges: 1 Carb, 1 Medium-Fat Meat & 1 Fat

► FACTS YOU SHOULD KNOW ABOUT TYPE 2 DIABETES

TYPE 2 DIABETES

Type 2 diabetes affects approximately 15 million Americans, or about 90 percent of the diabetes population. Interestingly, one-half of all people with type 2 diabetes are unaware that they have the disease. Unfortunately, diabetes is the sixth leading cause of death from disease in the United States.

WHO IS AT RISK FOR TYPE 2 DIABETES

Type 2 diabetes occurs for different reasons. In some people, the pancreas still produces insulin, sometimes at high levels, but the body doesn't use it efficiently. Genetics and ethnic background both play a major role in the development of type 2 diabetes. Other common factors are obesity, physical inactivity and older age.

WHAT IS INSULIN RESISTANCE?

One fundamental problem of type 2 diabetes is not a lack of insulin, but rather the body's failure to respond properly to its own insulin — which is called insulin resistance. Insulin resistance often appears before the rise in blood sugar marks the onset of type 2 diabetes. The good news is that medications are available that directly target insulin resistance.

DIABETES TREATMENT PLAN

Proper nutrition and physical activity, along with good blood sugar control and treating insulin resistance, are cornerstones of managing type 2 diabetes. Glitazones (insulin sensitizers), such as Avandia® (rosiglitazone maleate), treat an underlying cause of type 2 diabetes, insulin resistance, and improve blood sugar control. *Avandia* works by making the cells in your body more sensitive to your own natural insulin. Insulin sensitizers, given their unique mechanism of action, may have the potential to protect the insulin producing cells of the pancreas, thereby delaying the progression of the disease. Speak with your physician to learn more about managing diabetes.

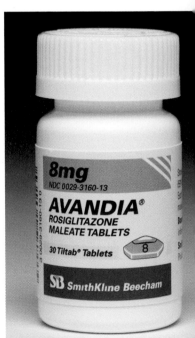

86

Please see the accompanying patient prescribing information that follows on page 88.

▶ GLOSSARY

Type 2 Diabetes — Condition where the pancreas does not produce enough insulin or the body cells are resistant to the action of insulin. Type 2 diabetes is the most common form of diabetes and in the past was referred to as "adult-onset diabetes."

Type 1 Diabetes — Condition when the pancreas makes little or no insulin because the beta cells have been destroyed. This form of diabetes is often known as "juvenile diabetes."

Avandia® (rosiglitazone maleate) — An oral medication for type 2 diabetes that directly targets insulin resistance, an underlying cause of the disease. A member of the glitazone drug class.

Glitazone (Thiazolidinedione) — The newest class of drugs for type 2 diabetes that turn insulin-resistant cells into insulin-sensitive cells, thereby allowing for more efficient use of the body's naturally produced insulin. Glitazones are insulin sensitizers.

Insulin — A hormone produced by the pancreas that helps the body use glucose for energy.

Blood Glucose (blood sugar) — The main sugar in the blood that the body makes from the three elements of food — proteins, fats and carbohydrates. Glucose is the major source of energy for living cells and is carried to each cell through the bloodstream.

Insulin Resistance — Condition when the body does not respond properly to its own insulin.

Fasting Blood Glucose Test (FBG) — Method for determining how much glucose is in the blood. This test is done to diagnose if a person has diabetes. The FBG test measures the amount of glucose in your blood after 12 hours or one night of not eating.

Hemoglobin A (HbA1c) — A blood test that measures a patient's average blood sugar over the previous two to three months. An important test for patients with diabetes to help physicians determine if their blood sugar is under control and determine if a change in medication is needed.

Meal Plan — A guide that details how much and what kinds of food you can choose to eat at meals and snack times.

Exchanges — Food groups used in lists for meal planning. There are seven basic groups: starch, fruit, milk, other carbohydrates, vegetables, meat and meat substitutes and fat. Any food in a given group can be exchanged for any other food in that same group in the appropriate amount.

87

Patient Information About AVANDIA®
(rosiglitazone maleate) Tablets
2 mg, 4 mg, and 8 mg

What is Avandia?

Avandia is one product in a new class of prescription drugs called thiazolidinediones (thigh-a-zoe-lid-een-die-owns). It is used to treat type 2 diabetes by helping the body use the insulin that it is already making. *Avandia* comes as pills that can be taken either once a day or twice a day to help improve blood sugar levels.

How does Avandia treat type 2 diabetes?

If you have type 2 diabetes, your body still produces insulin but it is not able to fully use the insulin. Insulin is needed to allow sugar to be carried from the bloodstream into many cells of the body for energy. If insulin is not being used correctly, sugar does not enter the cells very well and builds up in the blood. If not controlled, the high blood sugar level can lead to serious medical problems, including kidney damage, blindness and amputation.

Avandia helps your body use insulin by making the cells more sensitive to insulin so that the sugar can enter the cell.

How quickly will Avandia begin to work?

Avandia begins to reduce blood sugar levels within 2 weeks. However, since *Avandia* works to address an important underlying cause of type 2 diabetes, insulin resistance, it may take up to 12 weeks to see the full effect. If you do not respond adequately to your starting dose of *Avandia*, your physician may increase your daily dose to improve your blood sugar control.

How should I take Avandia?

Your doctor may tell you to take *Avandia* once a day in the morning or twice a day in the morning and evening. It can be taken with or without meals. Food does not affect how *Avandia* works. To help you remember to take *Avandia*, you may want to take it at the same time every day.

What if I miss a dose?

If your doctor has prescribed *Avandia* for use once a day:

- As soon as you remember your missed dose, take one tablet anytime during the day.

- If you forget and go a whole day without taking a dose, don't try to make it up by adding another dose on the following day. Forget about the missed dose and simply follow your normal schedule.

If your doctor has prescribed *Avandia* for use twice a day:

- As soon as you remember the missed dose, take one tablet.

- Take the next dose at the normal time on the same day.

- Don't try to make up a missed dose from the day before.

- You should never take three doses on any single day in order to make up for a missed dose the day before.

Do I need to test my blood for sugar while using Avandia?

Yes, you should follow your doctor's instructions about your at-home testing schedule.

Does Avandia cure type 2 diabetes?

Currently there is no cure for diabetes. The only way to avoid the effects of the disease is to maintain good blood sugar control by following your doctor's advice for diet, exercise, weight control, and medication. *Avandia*, alone or in combination with other prescription drugs, may improve these other efforts by helping your body make better use of the insulin it already produces.

Can I take Avandia with other medications?

Avandia has been taken safely by people using other medications including other antidiabetic medications, birth control pills, warfarin (a blood thinner), Zantac® (ranitidine, an antiulcer product manufactured by Glaxo Wellcome Inc.), certain heart medications, and some cholesterol-lowering products. You should discuss with your doctor the most appropriate plan for you. If you are taking prescription or over-the-counter products for your diabetes or for conditions other than diabetes, be sure to tell your doctor. Sometimes a patient who is taking two antidiabetic medications each day can become irritable, lightheaded or excessively tired. Tell your doctor if this occurs; your blood sugar levels may be dropping too low, and the dose of your medication may need to be reduced.

What should I discuss with my doctor before taking Avandia?

You should talk to your doctor if you have a history of edema, liver problems or congestive heart failure, or if you are nursing, pregnant or thinking of becoming pregnant. If you are a premenopausal woman who is not ovulating, you should know that *Avandia* therapy may result in the resumption of ovulation, which may increase your chances of becoming pregnant. Therefore, you may need to consider birth control options.

What are the possible side effects of Avandia?

Avandia was generally well tolerated in clinical trials. The most common side effects reported by people taking *Avandia* were upper respiratory infection and headache. As with most other diabetes medications, you may experience an increase in weight (3 to 8 pounds). This often occurs with improved blood sugar control. *Avandia* may also cause edema and/or anemia. If you experience any swelling of your extremities (e.g., legs, ankles) or tiredness, notify your doctor. Talk to your doctor if you experience shortness of breath or unusually rapid increase in weight.

Who should not use Avandia?

The following people should not take *Avandia*: People with type 1 diabetes, people who experience yellowing of the skin with Rezulin® (troglitazone, Parke-Davis), people who are allergic to *Avandia* or any of its components and people with diabetic ketoacidosis.

Why are laboratory tests recommended?

Your doctor may conduct blood tests to measure your blood sugar control. In addition, your doctor may conduct liver enzyme tests. *Avandia* did not show signs of liver problems in studies. However, because a related drug (*Rezulin*) has been associated with such problems, and because *Avandia* has not been widely used, your doctor may recommend a blood test to monitor your liver before you start taking *Avandia*, every 2 months during the first year and periodically thereafter.

It is important that you call your doctor immediately if you experience nausea, vomiting, stomach pain, tiredness, anorexia, dark urine, or yellowing of the skin.

How should I store Avandia?

Avandia should be stored at room temperature in a childproof container out of the reach of children. Store *Avandia* in its original container.

DATE OF ISSUANCE MAY 2000

©SmithKline Beecham, 2000

SmithKline Beecham Pharmaceuticals
Philadelphia, PA 19101

AV:L4PI   Printed in U.S.A.

▶ TOOLS & RESOURCES

NATIONAL ORGANIZATIONS

American Association of Diabetes Educators
Represents healthcare professionals who provide diabetes education and care.
100 West Monroe St. Suite 400
Chicago, IL 60611
800-832-6874
800-TEAMUP4 (for names of diabetes educators in your area)

American Diabetes Association
Provides research, information and advocacy for people with diabetes.
Attn: Customer Service
1701 N. Beauregard St.
Alexandria, VA 22311
800-DIABETES (800-342-2383)

National Diabetes Information Clearinghouse
Offers diabetes information to health professionals, patients and the general public.
1 Information Way
Bethesda, MD 20892-3560
800-GET LEVEL (800-438-5383)
301-654-3327

American Dietetic Association National Center for Nutrition and Dietetics
Provides nutrition and dietetic information and resources.
216 W. Jackson Blvd. Ste. 800
Chicago , IL 60606-6995
312-899-0040
800-877-1600
800-366-1655 (Consumer Nutrition Hotline)

American Heart Association National Center
Provides information on fighting heart disease and stroke.
7272 Greenville Ave.
Dallas, TX 75231
214-373-6300

Indian Health Service Diabetes Program
Provides health services, including diabetes information, to American Indians.
5300 Homestead Road, N.E.
Albuquerque, NM 87110
505-248-4182

International Diabetic Athletes Association
Includes persons with diabetes who participate in fitness activities and anyone interested in the relationship between diabetes and sports.
1647-B West Bethany Home Road
Phoenix, AZ 85015
800-898-IDAA
602-433-2113

WEBSITES

American Diabetes Association
www.diabetes.org

Centers for Disease Control and Prevention
http://www.cdc.gov/diabetes

Diabetes Monitor
www.diabetesmonitor.com

Diabetes.Com
www.diabetes.com

Diabetes Website
www.diabeteswebsite.com

Diabetes Control Center
www.dr-diabetes.com

National Diabetes Information Clearinghouse
www.niddk.nih.gov/health/diabetes/ndic.htm

For more information on Avandia® (rosiglitazone maleate), SmithKline Beecham Pharmaceuticals or for complete prescribing information, visit *Avandia* on the World Wide Web at **www.avandia.com**, or call 1-800-AVANDIA.

▶ THE INGREDIENTS FOR MANAGING TYPE 2 DIABETES

Developing a nutritional plan is as important as insulin, oral agents or exercise in the treatment of diabetes. A healthy and balanced meal plan along with physical activity, blood sugar control and treating insulin resistance, an underlying cause of type 2 diabetes, are the cornerstones for diabetes management.

UNDERSTANDING NUTRITIONAL INFORMATION

- The Diabetes Food Pyramid below makes it easy to remember what kinds of foods to include in your meal plan.

- The pyramid has six sections and emphasizes a low-fat, high-fiber diet. The largest food group – grains, beans and starchy vegetables – is on the bottom. This tells you that you should eat more of these types of foods than of any others. The smallest group, which includes fats, is at the top. This means that you should eat very few servings of these foods.

The percent of fat and calories varies from person to person. Following is a general guideline for people with diabetes.

- Fats are considered the most concentrated source of calories. Your daily share of calories from fat should be 30 percent or less, with only 10 percent from saturated fat.

- Carbohydrates are used for quick energy. The suggested share of daily calories from this group should be between 50 to 60 percent, preferably in the form of whole grains.

- Protein is needed for the growth of cells. Your need for protein decreases with age. Protein should make up about 10 to 20 percent of your daily diet.

MEAL PLANNING

To help start meal planning, we have created a three day meal plan using recipes from this book. Each recipe in this book includes complete nutritional information to guide you through meal planning. Following are some helpful hints to use when developing your own meal plan:

- Eat a variety of foods each day.

- Schedule meal planning with exercise and medication so that the three can work together to lower blood sugar levels.

- Follow a low-fat, low-cholesterol, high-fiber diet.

- Talk to your physician or diabetes educator to help develop a healthy meal plan based on your individual needs.

- Monitor portion sizes to make sure meal plans are balanced.

- Use the Diabetes Food Pyramid to help guide your food choices.

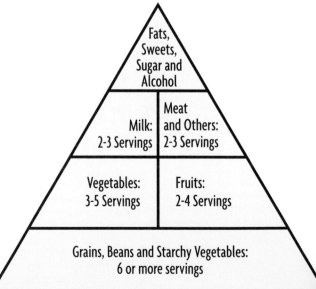

►A GUIDE FOR EATING

This is a sample meal plan and may not be appropriate for all individuals. Speak with your physician or dietitian about your individual needs. This sample 1,500 calorie meal plan is a guide for selecting meals using the recipes in this book.

	DAY 1	DAY 2	DAY 3
BREAKFAST	Scrambled Eggs with Cheese Grits 1 slice of toast 2 teaspoons of butter or margarine 1¼ cup of strawberries 1 cup of skim milk	¾ cup of cereal ½ small bagel ¾ cup of blueberries 1 cup of skim milk 2 tablespoons of light cream cheese	Mushroom, Goat Cheese and Herb Omelet 1 English muffin ½ banana ¾ cup of low-fat plain yogurt 1 teaspoon of butter or margarine 6 ounces of coffee or tea
LUNCH	Pueblo Squash Stew 6 unsalted crackers 2 ounces of grilled chicken ⅓ cantaloupe Sugar-free beverage	Asparagus Soup with Maine Lobster 24 oyster crackers New Potato and Green Bean Salad Sugar-free beverage	Shrimp and Eggplant Caponata 1 small roll 1 teaspoon of butter or margarine 1 small apple
SNACK	Coffee Amaretto Parfait 1 cup of skim milk	Famous Cocoa Wafer Stack with Raspberries	Baked Peaches with Vanilla Ice Cream
DINNER	Stir-Fried Fish with Sweet Peas ⅓ cup of rice Roasted Carrot Soup ¾ cup of pineapple Sugar-free beverage	Pan Roasted Chicken with Heirloom Tomatoes Butternut Squash Risotto 1 cup of tossed salad 2 tablespoons of salad dressing Sugar-free beverage	Seared Flank Steak Salad Grilled Portobello Mushroom 1 medium-sized baked potato
DAILY EXCHANGES	**Total Calories** 1459 **Total Carbohydrates** 177 grams **Protein** 82 grams **Fat** 47 grams **Calories from Fat** 29% **Calories from Carbs** 49% **Calories from Protein** 22%	**Total Calories** 1510 **Total Carbohydrates** 193 grams **Protein** 72 grams **Fat** 50 grams **Calories from Fat** 30% **Calories from Carbs** 51% **Calories from Protein** 19%	**Total Calories** 1480 **Total Carbohydrates** 188 grams **Protein** 74 grams **Fat** 48 grams **Calories from Fat** 29% **Calories from Carbs** 51% **Calories from Protein** 20%

▶ THE BENEFITS OF PHYSICAL ACTIVITY

Physical activity, along with good nutrition and medication, is key in the management of type 2 diabetes and is important for good diabetes control.

For people with diabetes, physical activity may:

- Lower blood sugar
- Help insulin work more efficiently
- Help decrease risk of complications associated with type 2 diabetes
- Lower HbA1c levels
- Burn fat
- Help to combat depression and reduce physical stress

Below are some tips on how to add physical activity into your day at home and at work:

- Climb one extra flight of stairs
- Walk eight extra minutes a day
- Walk down the hall instead of using the phone or e-mail
- Choose a lunch dining spot that is a 10-15 minute walk away
- Play with the kids
- Walk the dog
- Join a line dancing or ballroom dancing group
- Go to the park or zoo with family or friends
- Make a Saturday morning walk a family habit
- Do active outdoor chores: wash the car, mow the grass, garden
- Do active indoor chores: window washing, tub scrubbing, reorganize your closet

▶ INDEX

Written & Edited by Anthony Dias Blue

David Gadd, Associate Editor

THE RECIPE CONSULTANTS

Michel Nischan, Executive Chef,
Heartbeat Restaurant, New York

Dina Hulbert, R.D., CDE,
Diabetes Educator & Nutritionist

Gina Miraglia, Recipe Tester

THE REGIONAL CHEFS

Frank Brigtsen, Brigtsen's Restaurant,
New Orleans, Louisiana

Richard Chamberlain, Chamberlain's,
Dallas, Texas

Jack Czarnecki, The Joel Palmer House,
Dayton, Oregon

Tom Douglas, Dahlia Lounge, Palace Kitchen
& Etta's Seafood, Seattle, Washington

Paco Duarte, Columbia Restaurant,
Tampa/Ybor City, Florida

Susan Feniger & Mary Sue Milliken,
Border Grill & Ciudad, Los Angeles,
California

Emily Luchetti, Farallon,
San Francisco, California

Scott Newman, Rubicon,
San Francisco, California

Ken Oringer, Clio,
Boston, Massachusetts

Harlan Peterson, Tapawingo,
Ellsworth, Michigan

Marcus Samuelsson, Aquavit,
Minneapolis, Minnesota

Mark Tarbell, Tarbell's & Barmouche,
Phoenix, Arizona

Marc Vetri, Vetri's, Philadelphia, Pennsylvania

Martin Yan, Foster City, California

THE CREATIVE TEAM

Joel Avirom, Book Design and Art Direction

Jason Snyder and Meghan Day Healey,
Design Assistants

Marc Iorio, Contributing Writer

John Montana, Photography

Mike Moreno, Photography Assistant

Dyne Benner, Food Stylist

Maggie Ruggerio, Assistant Food Stylist

Elizabeth Engelhardt, Prop Stylist

Published by RR Donnelley & Sons Company
99 Park Avenue
New York, NY 10016